B. P. Pratten

Chisholm's All Round Route and Panoramic Guide of the St. Lawrence

B. P. Pratten

Chisholm's All Round Route and Panoramic Guide of the St. Lawrence

ISBN/EAN: 9783337149505

Printed in Europe, USA, Canada, Australia, Japan

Cover: Foto ©Andreas Hilbeck / pixelio.de

More available books at **www.hansebooks.com**

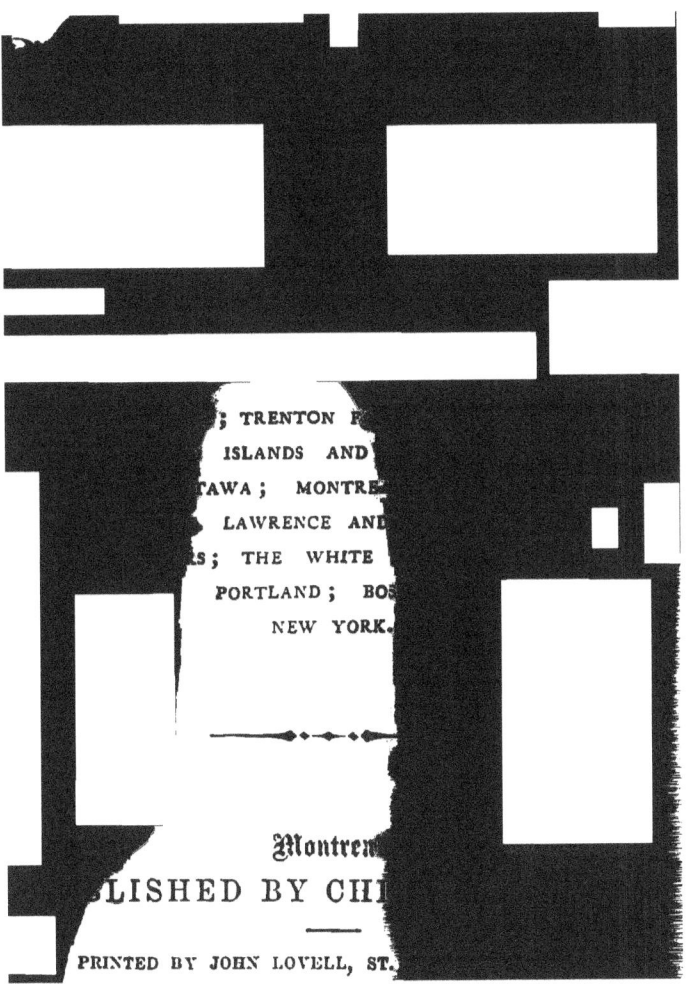

; TRENTON F
ISLANDS AND
AWA ; MONTRE
LAWRENCE AND
S ; THE WHITE
PORTLAND ; BO
NEW YORK.

𝔐ontre
LISHED BY CH

PRINTED BY JOHN LOVELL, ST.

PREFACE.

A Panoramic Guide of the "St. Lawrence" appears this season under a somewhat altered title, in an improved dress and enlarged form. It has absorbed the popular book known as the "All Round Route Guide," and, in order to meet the wants of the pleasure travel, the additional matter, taking in the various places of interest comprised in that work, has been added. Neither labour nor expense have been spared to make this a thoroughly reliable and attractive guide for tourists visiting the far-famed summer resorts, and the proprietors seek for the approval and patronage of an appreciative public.

In its new form, this guide will meet with the criticism of American tourists, and it is earnestly requested that any improvements, or alterations, that will benefit the work, may be communicated by those into whose hands it may fall, best able to make such suggestions. Additions, both in matter and illustrations, will be made, from year to year, and every effort made to make this what is really wanted, *a perfect Guide* and Handbook of the

ST. LAWRENCE.

THE HUDSON RIVER.

The scenery of the Hudson River has been so often written and talked about, that all who have never yet passed up its varied course, will, we presume, on starting on a trip of pleasure, endeavour to make acquaintance with a district that is not only beautiful to the eye, but has been the scene of many of those bloody actions between the Americans, (while yet struggling for their independence,) and the troops of Great Britain, before the yoke of sovereignty had been fairly broken.

We imagine, therefore, that this trip will be taken by daylight, and we recommend to the notice of our readers, the splendid steamers "Chauncey Vibbard" and "Daniel Drew," of the Day-line of Steamers. These are indeed floating palaces, for the speed and arrangements of the vessels, and the luxurious fittings of the saloons, are not surpassed by any other line of boats on the

"CHAUNCEY VIBBARD."

"Drew,"— are equally fine boats, and in their appointments unsurpassed by any steamers in the world. As they make the trip by night the scenery cannot be enjoyed to the fullest extent, yet a sail on the beautiful waters of the " Hudson " by moonlight is magnificent. The day steamers leave the wharf at Desbrosses street every morning at 8.A.M., calling at the foot of 34th street a quarter of an hour later, and run up the 150 miles of the Hudson by 6 o'clock in the evening.

For the first twelve miles of our upward journey we skirt along the Island of Manhattan, upon which the City of New York is built. One of the first objects of interest we see on the right hand, is the handsome stone edifice of the New York Orphan Asylum, where nearly 200 children of both sexes are clothed, fed, and taught, and ultimately assisted to find respectable employment in the world. The happy and contented locks of these poor children are, perhaps, the most satisfactory proofs of the success of this inestimable institution, which, founded in 1806, by several benevolent ladies, has, little by little, progressed, until we find it now occupying the stately and comfortable house whose gardens stretch down to the very edge of the water.

On the opposite side of the river, we pass by the yet picturesque villages of Hoboken and Weehawken. We say yet picturesque, as their close proximity to that city of cities, which is daily travelling onwards, would make one imagine that the villas and street palaces of its merchants would spoil their rural beauty; but this is not so. How long this state of things may remain it is impossible to conjecture, as lager beer saloons, pleasure gardens, and restaurants are daily being raised here.

Just above Manhattanville, a small village, and, one of the suburbs of New York, chiefly occupied by the poorer class of people, is Trinity Cemetery, where, among many others, lies Audubon, the celebrated naturalist, who has also given the name to a small village of about twenty or thirty acres where he used to live, but which, since his death, has been cut up into building lots, and still retains the aristocratic name of Audubon Park. Just beyond this park a large building, surmounted by a cupola, and having a tower at the south-west angle, may be descried among the trees. This is the New York Institution for the Deaf and Dumb, which under the skilful management of Mr. Peek, is probably unequalled by any similar establishment in America. It stands in its own grounds of thirty-seven acres, and the terrace upon which the buildings (five in number, arranged in a quadrangle) are erected is one hundred and thirty feet above the river. This Institution alone accommodates four hundred and fifty patients, and is only one more instance of the open-handed liberality and discriminating foresight of those in the State of New York, who do their best to alleviate distress in whatever form it may appear among their fellow creatures.

We here approach, on the same side, Fort Washington, or Washington Heights, as it is sometimes, and perhaps more appropriately, called. The ground is from five to six hundred feet above the river, and the view from this spot is exceedingly fine the eye being able to trace the windings of the Hudson River northward for many miles, whilst southward the great city we have just left, with its suburbs of Brooklyn and Jersey City, can be plainly seen, though ten miles off.

We now leave the Island of Manhattan behind us, having by this time passed abreast of the Spuyten Duyvil Creek, which separates the Island from the rest of the State of New York. The Hudson River Railroad crosses the creek by a long bridge, laid upon piles, and a station, called after the name of the inlet, is immediately on the other side of the bridge. On the opposite shore of the river that singularly beautiful formation of rock called "The Palisades," commences about here. They extend for nearly thirty-six miles, and are considered by many as the most interesting feature in the scenery. Commencing at Hoboken, this threatening ridge can be discerned as far as the Hook, towering as it were over the river to a height varying from three to five hundred feet, and the apparently columnar structure, as seen at a distance forcibly reminds one of the far-famed Fingal's Cave.

About two miles and a-half above Spuyten Duyvil, the tourist will perceive a handsome stone castellated building. This was dence, and is called Fonthill. It has now changed hands, and is a portion of the building belonging to the Convent and Academy of Mount St. Vincent, as the surrounding neighbourhood is called, having a station on the Hudson River Railway. Two miles higher up, we come to the flourishing village of Yonkers, near to which the little Sawmill River runs into the Hudson. The whole valley through which the Sawmill River runs is very beautiful, and the angler will find the stream well stocked with fish.

Four miles more steaming through a strikingly picturesque country brings us to Hastings and Dobb's Ferry, at both of which places the Railroad, which runs along the river, has stations. The division between the States of New Jersey and New York strikes the river on the left bank, just opposite Dobb's Ferry, and henceforth our journey is continued entirely through the State of New York.

We now approach a part of the river [that has associa]tions to both the American and British [nations. It was at] Tarrytown and Tappan, on the occasion of [] the rebellion of 1789, that Major [André] was hanged as a spy, after having [obtained] plans by which West Point could [be betrayed by] Arnold, of Washington's Army, [] Major André, who to the last m[] bravery, terminated his life as a s[oldier doing his] best to deliver his country into th[] death by placing himself under t[] Major André's body, after lying i[] fate for forty years, was at last give[n up] now finds a resting place among the [] Britain in Westminster Abbey.

The neighbouring district of TARRYTOWN and IRVINGTON is rich in associations of that greatest of American authors, Washington Irving. About half-a-mile above Irvington, on the right hand side of the river, may be seen, peeping through the bower of trees that nearly hides it from view, the charming stone cottage, called

"Sunnyside," the home of Washington Irving, and the place where most of his novels were written. The cottage was from time to time increased and improved whenever Irving had the means to do it, and it has now become naturally one of the chief objects of interest in the neighbourhood. Many other beautiful estates are to be seen around, and if time is a matter of no moment, we can well advise the traveller to stop here and [illegible] some hours.

Half-w[illegible]se
to the r[illegible]ilt
by the [illegible]is,
an arc[illegible]to
Tarryt[illegible]s
snugly[illegible]s.
We le[illegible]e,
which [illegible]e
here.

At S[illegible] [illegible]os-sibly exhibit less anxiety to tarry awhile, for, as [illegible], it is the seat of the Mount Pleasant Prison, belonging to the State of New York. The village itself contains about five thousand inhabitants, and is nearly two hundred feet above the river. The prison is built near the river; that for males being on the lower stage, whilst the building for females is higher up the slope. It has been completed since 1830, and can accommodate over a thousand persons, the buildings having from time to time been increased, as more room was needed.

Immediately opposite SING-SING, the Rockland Lake Ice Company have their depot, and employ a large number of men each winter to cut and store ice for the coming summer's consumption in New York. It is curious to note that whereas New York is almost entirely supplied with ice from this neighbourhood, it is also supplied with water from the Croton Lake, which is hard by. This lake is estimated to contain over six hundred million gallons of water, and (daily) fifty to sixty million gallons are contributed by it to supply New York with this necessary of life. The water is conveyed from this Lake, which is chiefly formed by a long DAM being built across it, through an aqueduct thirty-three miles long, right up to New York. The entire cost of this aqueduct was twelve million dollars. It is built of stone, brick, and cement, arched above and below, seven feet eight inches wide at the top, and six feet three inches at the bottom, the side walls being eight feet five inches high. A few more miles' travelling takes us past the small village of Haverstraw, which gives its name to the lovely bay, and then past a limestone quarry, extending along the bank for more than half-a-mile, and two hundred feet in height, and which must prove, from the number of men we can see employed in it, a very profitable speculation. Two miles further on, on the western side of the river, is Grassy Point, a small village where bricks are made, and, again, one mile higher up, is Stony Point, where there is a redoubt of considerable extent,—another one on the opposite side, at Verplank's Point, guarding the entrance to what is called the " Lower Highlands."

Three miles above Stony Point is GIBRALTAR or CALDWELL'S LANDING. DUNDERBERG MOUNTAIN rises its towering head almost immediately in the rear of this spot. Directly opposite is Peekskill, a thriving village of some five or six thousand inhabitants. The river here makes a sudden bend to the west. This is called the Race, and the scenery from here for the next fifteen miles is unequalled in beauty. On the right we pass by a rock promontory, called Anthony's Nose, whilst on the left, or western side, we have the DUNDERBERG MOUNTAIN already alluded to. Anthony's Nose is thirteen hundred feet above the surface of the river. The Hudson River Railway has had to tunnel under the bottom of this mountain for a distance of two hundred feet. On the opposite side of the river, a large creek can be seen, where vessels of almost any size could anchor. The entrance to this creek is guarded on one side by Fort Clinton, and on the other by Fort Montgomery—the two so close to one another that rifle shots could be easily exchanged, Fort Montgomery being on the northern side and Fort Clinton on the lower. Almost immediately under the shadow, as it were, of the former fort, lies the picturesque little island of Iona, belonging to Dr. C. W. Grant, and covered in the summer time with vines and pear trees, in the successful culture of which the worthy Doctor is supposed to be unequalled.

A little way above Iona, and but half-a-mile below West Point, we come upon the Buttermilk Falls, caused by the flowing down of a small stream into the river below, and falling over the hill-side a hundred feet in as many yards. This fall, when increased by any late rains or swollen by freshets, well deserves the homely name by which it is known, the snow-white foam truly giving it the appearance of buttermilk.

Half-a-mile further up brings us to " COZZEN'S HOTEL DOCK " at West Point. Here the vessel on which we are travelling stops for a while, to land passengers who are anxious to remain a day or so at Cozzen's comfortable hotel. This, during the summer season, is a very favourite resort, and much crowded; travellers would do well to make use of the telegraph a day before-hand to bespeak accommodation, or they may find themselves disappointed on their arrival.

One mile more brings us to " WEST POINT " itself, the most lovely of all the lovely spots on the river. It is well known that the great Military Academy is situated here. Space will not enable us to enter very fully into a description of the course of instruction pursued here, suffice it to say that the fact of a young man having passed through the course, is a clear proof of his being an officer and a gentleman in its broadest sense. The traveller may well pass a few hours in this locality, and if he should happen to be acquainted with any of the professors or cadets in the Military College, he will be enabled to go over the buildings, different galleries, &c., and judge for himself as to whether the instruction and discipline kept up is not likely to produce some of the finest military men—soldiers that any European nation might be proud of. Reluctantly we must draw ourselves away from West Point, and allow our steamer to plough her way once more along the flowing current, and between the shady and overhanging cliffs which give so much character to the scene at this spot. A very few revolutions of the wheel will bring us between the BOTERBERG MOUNTAIN on the western side, and the rock called BREAKNECK on the eastern bank, forming an imposing entrance to NEWBURGH BAY, from which a series of mountains, hills and cliffs rise in succession until they seem almost to shut out all remaining nature, and to give the idea that one is at the bottom of a large basin, from which there is no possible exit. CROWNEST is the principal of these mountains, rising almost directly from the river bank to a height of nearly one thousand five hundred feet. As the side of this mountain is entirely covered with foliage, the view of it in the summer time is most beautiful, and only to be exceeded by the sight of it in the commencement of October, when the fall tints are in their richest and most luxuriant profusion. Soon after passing between the two rocks, we come to a small town called CORNWALL, on the western shore. This is a place of very general resort in summer, and is much noted for its many pleasant drives and walks. Its nearness to the river and to West Point, makes it a very favourite place for travellers to spend some few days, whilst many stay here a very much longer time during the warm weather.

Between CORNWALL and NEWBURGH lies the once prosperous but now sadly decayed settlement of NEW WINDSOR. It is now almost entirely a collection of small houses in great want of repair. On the shore, but higher above it on the plateau, one can discover several large farms with comfortable houses attached, giving the idea that if there is decay below there is no want of plenty above. Leaving this tumble-down village either to be repaired, or to fall into still greater decay, we will approach the more flourishing town of NEWBURGH, where the steamer stops for a few minutes to discharge some of her passengers and to take up others, and we will employ these few minutes in gazing at the substantial streets and houses of the town, which, by the by, we should have designated a city, seeing that it boasts of a mayor and corporation of its own. The first settlement at NEWBURGH was made as early as 1709, by some emigrants from the Palatinate ; since then, English, Irish, Welsh, Scotch, and Germans have followed their example, but of all these varied nationalities the Scotch have, perhaps, done the most towards making the place what it is. The brewery of

Mr. Beveridge is situated here, where ales are made which are known all over the country, and, on a hot day, are certainly a most acceptable "beverage." Among the other large stores is an extensive flannel factory, in which a very large number of hands are daily employed.

Exactly opposite NEWBURGH is the more modest looking village of FISHKILL LANDING, from which place any traveller anxious to ascend the South Beacon hill can do so with the assistance of any of the boy guides to be picked up in the streets of the village; and let us tell the traveller that he had better avail himself of our advice and take a guide, or before he reaches the top he may have repented of not having done so, as it is quite easy to lose oneself in the numerous gorges and ravines that are about the summit of the Beacon. As this is one of the highest mountains about here, the view from the top is most extensive and interesting. Far up to the north the Catskill mountains can be discerned, while to the east the Shawangunk hills are to be seen. Southwards, again, Boterberg and Breakneck, already seen, guard the pass through which the river running at our feet finds its way down to the sea. But it is time that we should descend from our lofty position and go on our way up the river.

A broad rocky platform, jutting out into the river, cannot fail to attract the traveller's attention. This is called the DEVIL'S DANSKAMMER, or Dancing Chamber, and, down to a comparatively late date, was used by the Indians as the scene of some of their religious ceremonies.

For about the next five miles we steam on through pretty country, though without finding anything striking enough to draw attention, until we pass the little village of NEW HAMBURG, lying at the mouth of WAPPINGER CREEK, which is navigable for some distance up. The railroad crosses the Wappinger by a causeway and drawbridge, and then pierces a promontory jutting out into the river, by a tunnel about eight hundred feet long. New Hamburg is a pretty little village, but nothing more. About a mile higher up, and on the opposite side of the river, is another small village called HAMPTON, then comes MARLBOROUGH two miles higher up still, with BARNEGAT nearly opposite, on the right hand side, and again MILTON LANDING two miles more on the left hand side. As these villages lie mostly on the high banks of the river there is not much to be seen of them from the boats, but they act as outlets or ports to the country districts lying behind them, and, judging from

VIEW ON THE HUDSON.

the numerous comfortable-looking country-houses in their immediate neighbourhood, must be tolerably thriving.

As already stated, these villages are hardly important enough to require mention, but we now approach a town of some twenty thousand inhabitants, rejoicing in the peculiar name of Poughkeepsie, and nearly half-way between New York and Albany, being seventy-five miles from the former, and about seventy from the capital of the State through which we are passing. It was formerly settled by the Dutch, towards the close of the seventeenth century, and is situated, like most of their river cities, at the mouth of a tributary stream or creek. The village, as it was then, has much extended, and now occupies the large open plain about two hundred feet above the river. The streets are broad, handsome, and well planted with trees, affording in summer grateful shelter from the piercing rays of the sun. Poughkeepsie is best known for the very excellent schools it maintains, a large boarding-school for boys upon College Hill being particularly renowned for the very excellent tuition imparted to the scholars. This building stands at the back of the city, about seven hundred feet above the river, and is a conspicuous object as seen from the water.

Six miles above Poughkeepsie, after a sudden bend in the river, we come upon some rocky and precipitous banks. This used to be called by the original settlers "Krom Elleboge," but has since been Anglicised into "CRUM ELBOW." Quite close to this, only high up from the river, stands the village of HYDE-PARK, called after a former Governor of the State of New York, Sir Edward Hyde, who, we regret to say, did not leave a very satisfactory reputation behind him ; his tyrannical and unprincipled conduct.is well known to all who have studied the history of New York when under British rule.

RHINEBECK LANDING lies about two miles away from the village of the same name, which was first settled by one William Beckman, a German, who came from the neighbourhood of the Rhine, and called the place partly in honour of his birthplace and partly after himself. Immediately opposite Rhinebeck Landing, across the river, is KINGSTON'S LANDING, a quiet little village, pleasant enough, but without any great activity apparent, though Kingston cement, which comes from here, is in much request. Between this and Hudson, fifteen miles off, we come upon a number of large, substantially built and handsome country houses, with lawns of smooth turf stretching down towards the river, and an air of luxury and wealth pervading the whole estates.

Six miles above RHINEBECK is BARRYTOWN, and four miles above Barrytown is TIVOLI, each of them possessing a station on the railroad, though, like many of the other villages we have had a glance at, small and unpretentious, having, however, possibly a vast idea of their own importance, as a great deal of the farm and garden produce of these villages is sent up to supply the wants of the Fifth Avenue, and other districts of the great city. Opposite Tivoli, on the western bank of the river, stands a flourishing little village called SAUGERTIES, at the mouth of the Esopus Creek. This little place boasts manufactories of iron, paper, and white-lead, and a fine flagstone quarry. Two miles from Saugerties we pass MALDEN, which lies backed by the Catskill Mountains, and about ten miles on we come to the large village of CATSKILL. Passengers from New York by railroad who wish to ascend the mountains, must alight at Catskill Station, and cross by ferry to the village, and we sincerely recommend our travellers to avail themselves of this trip. They will find plenty of omnibuses and stages to take them to the Mountain House, and the Clove, about twelve miles off. We shall not attempt to describe the scenery, which, at this point, must be seen to be appreciated. The Mountain House is built on a large platform, three thousand eight hundred feet above the level of the river, and can easily accommodate from two to three hundred guests. The view from this spot is of a most extensive character, and embraces a region of about ten thousand square miles in extent, portions even of Vermont, Massachusetts, and Connecticut being, on a fine day, plainly visible, whilst at least sixty miles of the Hudson River can be seen shining like a broad silver belt at our feet. Besides the Mountain House, the Falls must be visited, and we cannot do better than quote, and, what is more, endorse a paragraph which we find in "Miller's Guide to the Hudson River," and to which book we are indebted for much valuable and interesting information with regard to this locality.

" The odious showman spirit that spoils so many attractive
" places the world over, has entered here, and turns the Falls on
" or off according to the amount of sixpences forthcoming from

"lovers of what, considering the smallness of the stream when at "its best, may be called pitcher-esque. But the Clove, or Cleft, "down which the stream runs to the Hudson, is really wild and "savage, and romantic enough for the most ardent lover of such "rough scenery. These Falls are the outlets of two ponds far up "the mountain, united and leaping down a perpendicular rock in "two falls, one of one hundred and eighty feet, and another of "eighty feet in height, and emptying through the Clove, a deep "chasm into the plain below."

Five miles from Catskill Station, on the eastern side of the river, we come to the large and handsomely-built city of HUDSON, the chief town in Columbia County, one hundred and fifteen miles from New York, and thirty from Albany. The city is built on an eminence above the river, like many of the other villages we have passed in our course. The streets are wide and well laid out, and altogether the place has an air of thrift and prosperity. The principal street is called the Promenade, and laid out with trees and shrubs with excellent taste. One side is built with handsome houses, and the other is open to the river, and runs along the bank for nearly a mile. Any one anxious to pay a visit to the Shaker Village at Mount Lebanon had better leave the boat here and take the train which leaves for Chatham three times during the day, and there the traveller will connect with the Boston and Albany Railway, and, after an hour's journey of twenty-three miles, will be landed at the Shaker Village itself. Space will not allow an extended notice of this remarkable village; suffice it to say that cleanliness, and all the other cardinal virtues, reign paramount. Order, temperance, frugality, and Shaker worship, are the things that strike one's senses on first arriving. Every one here is free. No soldiers, no police, no judges live here, and among members of a society in which every man stakes his all, appeal to the courts of Law is a thing unknown. Among a sect where celibacy is the first and principal code, it would seem as if such a society would of itself die a natural death; but yearly many fresh converts to the sect are made, and not only among the old and those tired of this world's pomps and vanities, but from the young and healthy of both sexes. Happiness, peace and plenty are so evident in all the villages of this most peculiar of all religious societies, that it is not remarkable to hear that at the census of 1860 the Shakers were discovered to number from six to seven thousand, and at the present day they count considerably more. Mr. Hepworth Dixon has lately written so fully about them in his interesting work, entitled "New America," that we should recommend the curious, or those who have visited any of their villages, to obtain the book and "read them up."

We must go back to our steamer at Hudson, however, after this digression, and before leaving this interesting town may mention that the village opposite, which has the high-sounding name of Athens given to it (though for what cause we are ignorant) can be reached by a small steam ferry. There is nothing, however, to reward the task of crossing, except perhaps in order to obtain a good view of Hudson; but as this can be done quite as satisfactorily from the deck of our steamer, we will presume our readers will not attempt the passage, but continue with us for the next thirty miles of our trip to Albany.

The light-house seen on the western side of the river on FOUR MILE POINT, (that distance from Hudson) marks the head of navigation for ships. About a mile higher up, on the same side, is COXSACKIE VILLAGE, the older portion is called Coxsackie street, and lies on a large plain about a mile back from the river. NEW BALTIMORE and COEYMAN'S are two smaller settlements north of Coxsackie, with SCHODACK LANDING immediately on the other side, whilst four miles higher up is CASTLETON. Here the well known sand-bar, called the Overslaugh, is situated, a spot that has proved fatal to more steamboats and other vessels than any known place on the continent. The country just around here is flat, though apparently well cultivated. Soon after leaving this village we approach a place evidently of some importance, as the river has a busier look, and the banks are more thickly dotted with houses, and, after a few minutes' delay, we see in the distance the thickly built city of Albany, the Capital of the State, whilst the newly constructed railroad bridge which spans the river immediately opposite the city, seems to bar any further progress in our floating palace. We have now really reached the end of our water journey, unless we wish to proceed as far as Troy, when a little steam tender will come alongside of our stately craft, and if any passengers intend to go on, and so reach Montreal without passing to Niagara or Toronto, they can get on board, after having informed the Purser, who will see that their baggage accompanies them, and a half-hour's steam will take them on to Troy, where they can connect with the train leaving New York at 3.45 p.m., and reaching Troy at 10.00 p.m., engage their berth in the sleeping-car (which is put on to the train here) and find themselves in Montreal at about nine the next morning, after having enjoyed a refreshing and appetizing breakfast at the comfortable and handsomely fitted-up Restaurant in the newly-built Depôt at St Albans.

To those who are desirous of a more speedy transit between New York and Albany, we would say, that the Hudson River Railway, one of the best appointed roads in the world, skirts the eastern bank of the Hudson, and passengers can enjoy the scenery at a speed of 30 miles an hour, in one of that Company's elegant drawing-room cars.

As we wish to take our travellers to Montreal by the round-about, but more interesting route *via* Niagara, we will return to where we left them on the quay at Albany, after having landed them from the steamer which we have been reluctant to quit. If they wish to go on to Niagara the same night, they have not much time to waste, as the train leaves the depôt as soon as the passengers from the boats can be got there; and after a night's travel of about three hundred miles they will reach the Suspension Bridge Station at seven o'clock in the morning. Before leaving Albany, we ought, in justice to the city, to draw attention to the State House and the Dudley Observatory, about the only two buildings of any character in the whole place, and these two are not very likely to strike an observer dumb with admiration or astonishment on seeing them for the first time.

The view from the Capital is doubtless very fine, as the whole of the city, and a large tract of the surrounding country, can be

CITY OF ALBANY, N.Y.

seen from this eminence. Some of our travellers, who wish to take things easily, and rest a night or some few hours at Albany, will find themselves very comfortably put up at the " Delevan House," kept by Messrs. Charles G. Leland & Co. They can then take the train on the New York Central Railway for Utica, en route to

TRENTON FALLS.

As these Falls lie only about seventeen miles off the line of railway, with a branch railroad right up to them, they ought not to be passed without a visit. We will, therefore, take our seats in the cars at Albany, by the morning train, change at Utica, and either hire a conveyance there to take us on, or get into the cars which connect with this train, and bring us to the Trenton Falls Station a little after noon. The river forming the Trenton Falls is called the Canada Creek West, but, as this name is not euphonious and rather a mouthful, the Falls have been named after the town or parish in which they are situated. There is no one special cataract at Trenton which in itself is pre-eminently wonderful, grand or beautiful. It is more the position, form and rapidity of the river which give the charm, and make it considered by many as one of the most picturesque and lovely spots on the continent. As the usual passage for tourists is along the bed of the river itself, it can be understood that to see these falls aright there must not be too much water. The end of July, or the commencement of August, is the time to see them in all their beauty. In order to justify their name, there are two actual waterfalls here, which, within a few hours' journey from Niagara, or seen after that mightiest of all cataracts, would be merely considered as "squirts," but when taken on one's way to the Falls, and viewed in connection with the surrounding scenery, are well worthy of the visit we propose to make. The banks of the river are thickly wooded on each side with broken clefts here and there, through which the colors of the foliage show themselves, and straggling boughs and rough roots break

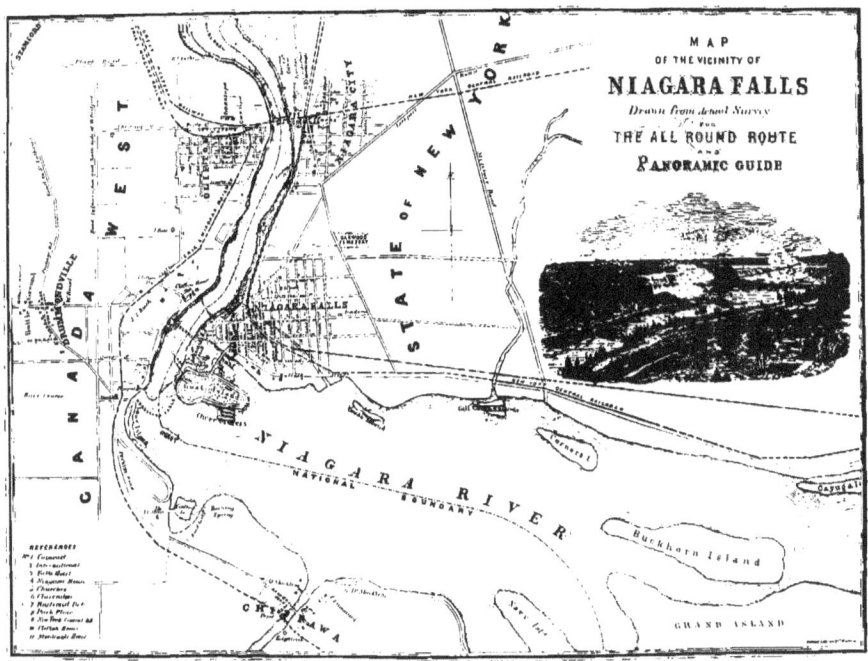

through the high rocks, and add to the wildness and charm of the scene

A comfortable hotel is situated in the village, where travellers can get all their wants supplied, and then take the cars at 3.45 p.m. back to UTICA, where they can again join the New York Central line, and proceed viâ ROME, SYRACUSE, ROCHESTER and LOCKPORT on their way to Niagara. As we presume that this journey will be made without any further stoppages, we shall skip all these places, and merely say that they are the ordinary specimens of American towns, having broad streets, avenues of trees, large stores, and excellent houses, with an air of prosperity about the whole of them.

NIAGARA.

Having landed our travellers safely at the Suspension Bridge Station of the New York Central Railway, the choice of an hotel is the matter of first and paramount importance. General opinion is much divided on this subject, many travellers asserting that the American side is the only one to stop on and see the Falls, as the Rapids, the Terrapin Tower and Goat Island are all to be reached from that side, and from that alone; whilst others take the broader view of the question that these minor sights ought to give place to the Falls, and therefore the only place to obtain an uninterrupted view of the two mighty cataracts is from the Canadian side. We are inclined to endorse this opinion, and therefore, if our travellers will be guided by us, we advise orders being given to the driver of the carriage, that can be engaged at the Station, to proceed to the "Clifton House" on the Canadian bank, kept by Messrs. Bromley & Shears. The drive from the Station to the "Clifton House" will necessitate the passage of the Suspension Bridge, and therefore, *en passant*, we will endeavor to give a short description of this wonderful triumph of engineering skill. The bridge is constructed for the joint purposes of road and pedestrian traffic, and for the Great Western Railway of Canada—the lower tier or floor being for foot and carriage passengers, whilst the upper portion is used entirely by the trains. There is a small toll levied on all passengers, and a custom-house officer will make a cursory and rapid search lest any articles liable for duty, are being carried across from the United States into the Dominion of Canada, or *vice versa*. ·Mr. Roebling, of Trenton, New Jersey, was the engineer of this Bridge, which, as the name implies, is constructed on the suspension system. The two towers supporting the entire structure, which is in one span (800 ft.), are about 80 feet high, and built on and into the solid rock; the aggregate length of wire employed is more than 4,000 miles, whilst the entire weight of the Bridge is 12,400 tons. From the centre of the tube or tunnel, the first view of the entire Falls can be seen, yet a mile and a-half distant: the never changing mist and spray dimly obscuring the view of the horse-shoe or Canadian Fall. The drive is continued along the high bank overlooking the foaming, seething waters of the river which have so lately made their giant leap. Almost immediately under the Bridge can be seen, at a distance down of about 250 feet, the wharf from which the small steamer, "Maid of the Mist," used to embark her passengers, before taking them up under the spray of the Falls. The successful escape of this little picture of a boat from the hands of the Sheriff, by taking the rapids and skimming through the whirlpool below, is now so much a matter of history that we will not weary our readers by detailing it again. Our task is now simply in as few words as possible to direct the tourist as to what to see, and how to see it. We will therefore imagine him to be standing in the balcony of the hotel overlooking the Falls, and explain to him that the right hand and larger cataract is the Canadian or Horse-Shoe Fall, whilst the one nearer to him, on the left hand side, is the American. The dimensions of the two Falls must necessarily be a matter of computation, and they are estimated as follows:

The American Fall, 900 feet across, with a drop of 164 feet.

The Canadian Fall, 1,900 feet across, with a drop of 158 feet.

The traveller in his first visit to this place is impressed with a sense of inexpressible amazement. His emotions are not unlike those of the votary of necromancy, who, when once within the magic circle, trembles under the influence of the enchanter, even before he confronts the wizard himself.

HORSE SHOE FALL.

Who can forget his first view of this grand and stupendous spectacle? The roaring is so tremendous, that it would seem that if all the lions that ever have lived since the days of Daniel, could join their voices in one " Hullah's " chorus, they would produce but a whisper, in comparison, to the deep diapason of this most majestic of all nature's pipes or organs.

HORSE SHOE FALL.

The wooden bridge which connects the mainland with Goat Island is eagerly passed, and we explore the whole of this curious crag, which is rightly named, for it is found fantastic enough to suggest that goats only could find a comfortable footing. The sublimity of the scene increases at every step; but when we come upon the mighty Cataract, we gaze in speechless wonder. But words cannot describe the grandeur of this scene, nor the emotions which it excites; neither can the pencil, any more than the pen, do it justice. The silent and the still picture wants the motion and the sound of that stupendous rush of waters. It is impossible to paint the ever rising column of spray that spires upward from the foaming gulf below, or the prismatic glory that crowns it; for there indeed has God forever

THE RAPIDS.

HORSE SHOE FALLS—FROM CANADA SIDE.

ALL ROUND ROUTE AND PANORAMIC GUIDE. 27

HORSE SHOE FALLS—FROM THE AMERICAN SIDE.

"set His bow" in the cloud, and cold must be the heart that in such a scene remembers not His covenant.

As neither descriptive language nor pictorial art can give an adequate conception of the magnitude of this wondrous Cataract, some notion may be suggested of the immense volume of water falling over the precipice, when it has been computed to be nearly 20,000,000 cubic feet per minute, in the Horse Shoe Fall alone; to say nothing of the Fall on the American side. It is calculated that these Falls recede at the rate of a foot every year. It is here that the beautiful phenomenon of the rainbow is seen to such advantage.

SUSPENSION BRIDGE ACROSS THE RIVER.

After much trouble and perseverance Mr. J. T. Bush obtained charters at Albany and Toronto for the new bridge, and commenced the work in 1867. On the 1st January, 1869, it was opened to the public. The capital stock of the bridge is $100,000, it has even cost something like $120,000. The bridge is located about 1,800 feet below the American falls on the American side, landing on the Canadian side only 8 or 10 rods below the Clifton House. The towers on the Canadian side are 120 feet high, and on the American side 106 feet high. The span is 1,230 feet from tower to tower. The height from the water to the floor of the bridge is 256 feet. There is a single track for carriages, and space at one side for foot passengers. The bridge has at each side a strong railing 5 feet high; the estimated strength of the structure is over 150 tons, and as 10 or 15 tons is all that could well be placed on the bridge at any one time by its ordinary traffic, the greatest confidence prevails as to its stability; added to this is the fact that the bridge passed through safely the gale of last November, which at Niagara was a perfect hurricane. The bridge stood without moving a plank through the 15 hours the gale lasted. It has now passed through two winters with its load of ice and frozen spray, so that it is no longer an experiment, but a fixed fact, and full confidence has been established.

NEW SUSPENSION BRIDGE

The bridge stands as a great lasting monument to J. T. Bush, who conceived the project and carried it to a successful termination.

The erection of this bridge brings Goat Island and Table Rock within easy walking distance. The view from the centre of it is exceedingly fine; suspended in mid-air—in full view of both the American and Horse Shoe Falls—the river above and below with its beautiful banks from 150 to 250 feet perpendicular, presents a view never before enjoyed by visitors to this wonderfully beautiful resort.

TABLE ROCK.

This was truly a magnificent crag,— the projection at the top being immense, from which large masses frequently fell. Many accidents have happened to tourists venturing too near the precipice. The Table Rock, however, exists now but in memory, for it suddenly gave way some years ago. Had this accident occurred an hour or two earlier in the day, the Victoria Bridge, the Grand Trunk Railway, and all other Canadian undertakings thereunto pertaining, would be a dream of the future and not a substantiality of the present; for a very short time previous to the disappearance of the slippery granite, there were standing upon it, viewing the Falls, the engineer of the Bridge, and several of his colleagues in the enterprises that have been mentioned.

ENTRANCE TO THE CAVE OF THE WINDS.

BURNING SPRING

Is about one mile above Table Rock, near the river's edge. The water of the spring is highly charged with sulphuretted hydrogen gas, and emits a pale, blue light, when ignited. To heighten the effect, the phenomenon of the burning water is exhibited in a darkened room.

TABLE ROCK—NIAGARA FALLS.

About three miles below the Falls is a frightfully wild spot, called the Whirlpool. The ravine is termed the Bloody Run, from a sanguinary engagement between two hostile Indian tribes. No human effort could possibly rescue the unfortunate individual who should happen to become entrangled in the eddies of this pool.

It is supposed that there is a subterraneous current from this spot. Between it and the Falls there was a temporary suspension bridge; but it has been superseded by the one for the Great Western Railway of Canada.

THE DEVIL'S HOLE

is a large triangular chasm in the bank of the river, three and a half miles below the Falls. The Bloody Run, as previously mentioned, falls into this chasm.

The following tale will, we think, be read with interest, in connection with Niagara:

THE HERMIT OF THE FALLS.

About twenty-five years since, in the glow of early summer, a young stranger of pleasing countenance and person made his appearance at Niagara. It was at first conjectured that he was an artist, a large portfolio, with books and musical instruments, being among his baggage. He was deeply impressed with the majesty and sublimity of the Cataract and the surrounding scenery, and expressed an intention to remain a week, that he might survey them at his leisure. But the fascination, which all minds of sensibility feel in the presence of that glorious work of the Creator, grew strongly upon him, and he was heard to say that six weeks were insufficient to become acquainted with its beauties. At the end of that period he was still unable to tear himself away, and desired to "build there a tabernacle," that he might indulge in his love of solitary musings, and admire at leisure the sublimity of nature. He applied for a spot on the Three Sisters' Island, on which to erect a cottage after his own model; one of the peculiarities of which was a drawbridge, to insure isolation. Circumstances forbidding compliance with this request, he took up his residence in an old house on Iris Island, which he rendered as comfortable as the state of the case would admit. Here he remained about eighteen months, when the intrusion of a family interrupted his habits of seclusion and meditation. He then quietly withdrew, and reared for himself a less commodious habitation near Prospect Point. When winter came, a cheerful fire of wood blazed upon the hearth, and he beguiled the long hours of evening by reading and music. It was strange to hear, in such a solitude, the long-drawn, thrilling notes of the viol, or the softest melody of the flute, gushing forth from that low-browed hut, or the guitar breathing out so lightly amid the rush and thunder of the never slumbering torrent. Though the world of letters was familiar to his mind, and the living world to his observation, for he had travelled widely, both in his native Europe and the East, he sought not association with mankind, to unfold or to increase his stores of knowledge. Those who had occasionally conversed with him, spoke with equal surprise and admiration of his colloquial powers, his command of language, and his fervid eloquence; but he seldom and sparingly admitted this intercourse, studiously avoiding society; though there seemed in his nature nothing of misanthropy or moroseness. On the contrary, he showed kindness to even the humblest animals. Birds instinctively learned this amiable trait in his character, and freely entered his dwelling, to receive from his hands crumbs or seeds.

But the absorbing delight of his solitary residence was communion with Niagara. Here he might be seen at every hour of the day or night, a fervent worshipper. At the gray dawn he went to visit it in the vail of mist; at noon, he banqueted in the full splendor of its glory; beneath the soft tinting of the lunar bow he lingered, looking for the angel whose pencil had painted it; and, at solemn midnight, he knelt at the same shrine. Neither the storms of autumn, nor the piercing cold of winter, prevented his visits to the temple of his adoration. There was, at this time, an extension of the Scrappin Bridge, by a single beam of timber, carried out ten feet over the fathomless abyss, where it hung tremulously, guarded only by a rude parapet. Along this beam he often passed and repassed, in the darkness of night. He even took pleasure in grasping it with his hands, and thus suspending himself over the awful gulf; so much had his morbid enthusiasm taught him to revel amid the terribly sublime. Among his favorite gratifications, was that of bathing, in which he indulged daily.

One bright but rather chilly day in the month of June, 1831, a man, employed about the ferry, saw him go into the water, and for a long time after observed his clothes to be still lying upon the bank. The poor hermit had taken his last bath. It was supposed that cramp might have been induced by the chill of the atmosphere or the water. Still the body was not found, the depth and force of the current below being exceedingly great. In the course of their search, they passed on to the Whirlpool. There, amid those boiling eddies, was the body, making fearful and rapid gyrations upon the face of the black waters. At some point of suction, it suddenly plunged and disappeared. Again emerging, it was fearful to see it leap half its length above the flood, then float motionless, as if exhausted, and, anon, spring upward, and seem to struggle like a maniac battling with a mortal foe. For days and nights this terrible scene was prolonged. It was not until the 21st of June, that, after many efforts, they were able to recover the body, and bear it to his desolate cottage. There they found his faithful dog, guarding the door. Heavily had the long period worn away, while he watched for his only friend, and wondered why he delayed his coming. He scrutinized the approaching group suspiciously, and would not willingly have given them admittance A stifled wail at length showed his intuitive knowledge of his master, whom the work of death had effectually disguised from the eyes of men. On the pillow was his pet kitten, and in different parts of the room were his guitar, flute, violin, portfolio and books, scattered,—the books open, as if recently used. It was a touching sight; the hermit mourned by his humble retainers, the poor animals that loved him, and ready to be laid by strange hands in a foreign grave.

The motives that led this singular and accomplished being, learned in the languages, in the arts and sciences, improved by extensive travel, and gifted with personal beauty and a feeling heart, to seclude himself, in the flower of youth, from human society, are still enveloped in mystery. All that is known, was, that his name was Francis Abbot, that he was a native of England, where his father was a clergyman, and that he had received from thence ample remittances for his comfort. These facts had been previously ascertained, but no written papers were found in his cell to throw additional light upon the obscurity in which he had so effectually wrapped the history of his pilgrimage.

Before leaving this place, we wish to conduct our readers to one spot where, perhaps, of all others, the finest view of the waterfalls can be seen, and that is along the railway tract that lies at the back of Mr. Zimmerman's house, until an open spot is reached near a small reservoir, immediately above the Falls, and as we feel that our language is too poor to give any adequate idea of the grandeur of the sight before us, we will take the liberty of reprinting the actual words in which that greatest of living writers, Mr. Charles Dickens, clothed his thoughts and feelings on his first visit to Niagara, twenty-eight years ago, and which, even now, with eight and twenty years' additional experience, he could not improve upon, either in force or poetic sentiment :—

" When we were seated in the little ferry-boat, and were crossing
" the swollen river immediately before both cataracts, I began to
" feel what it was : but I was in a manner stunned, and unable to
" comprehend the vastness of the scene. It was not until I came
" on Table Rock and looked—Great Heaven—on what a fall of

"bright green water!—that it came upon me in its full might and majesty.

"Then, when I felt how near to my Creator I was standing, the first effect, and the enduring one—instant and lasting—of the tremendous spectacle was Peace. Peace of Mind—Tranquillity—calm recollections of the Dead: Great thoughts of Eternal Rest and Happiness—nothing of Gloom or Terror. Niagara was at once stamped upon my heart, an Image of Beauty to remain there changeless and indelible until its pulses cease to beat forever.

"I never stirred in all that time from the Canadian side, whither I had gone at first. I never crossed the river again; for I knew there were people on the other shore, and in such a place it is natural to shun strange company. To wander to and fro all day, and see the cataracts from all points of view, to stand upon the edge of the great Horse-shoe Fall, marking the hurried water gathering strength as it approached the verge, yet seeming, too, to pause before it shot into the gulf below; to gaze from the river's level up to the torrent as it came streaming down; to climb the neighboring heights and watch it through the trees, and see the wreathing water in the Rapids hurrying on to take its fearful plunge; to linger in the shadow of the solemn rocks three miles below, watching the river as, stirred by no visible cause, it heaved and eddied and awoke the echoes, being troubled yet, far down beneath the surface, by its giant leap; to have Niagara before me, lighted by the sun and by the moon, red in the day's decline and gray as evening slowly fell upon it, to look upon it every day, and wake up in the night, and hear its ceaseless voice—this was enough.

"I think in every quiet season now, still do those waters roll and leap, and roar and tumble all day long; still are the rainbows spanning them a hundred feet below. Still, when the sun is on them, do they shine and glow like molten gold. Still, when the day is gloomy, do they fall like snow, or seem to crumble away like the front of a great chalk cliff, or roll down the rock like dense white smoke. But always does the mighty stream appear to die as it comes down, and always from the unfathomable grave arises

" that tremendous ghost of spray and mist which is never laid,
" which has haunted this place with the same dread solemnity
" since darkness brooded on the deep, and that first flood before
" the deluge—Light—came rushing on creation, at the Word of
" God."

NIAGARA CITY.

From the beautiful view here obtained of the Falls this place was formerly called Bellevue. The village has mostly grown up since the time of the erection of the Suspension Bridge at this point. A grist mill has been erected near the Bridge, the water-wheel of which is placed beneath, requiring a shaft 280 feet long to communicate with the mill, on the top of the bank. The town contains many fine buildings; prominent among these is a very large Railroad Depot. Niagara City has grown so rapidly, and is still so much upon the increase, that a general description only can be applied to it for any length of time.

LEWISTON.

This village is situated at the head of navigation, on the Lower Niagara, and is a place of considerable importance. It lies three miles below the Devil's Hole, and seven miles below the Falls at the foot of the mountain.

It is an exceedingly pleasant and very well built village, but its commercial prospects have been very much injured by the construction of the Erie and Welland Canals. It contains, besides a proportionate number of stores and hotels, churches of all the various denominations, and an academy of considerable size. In 1812, it was the head quarters of General Van Rensslaer, of the New York Militia.

QEEENSTON.

This is a small village, situated nearly opposite to Lewiston, and contains about 200 inhabitants. It is the Canadian termination of the Bridge, and is associated in history with the gallant defence made by the British, on the adjacent heights, in the war of 1812. The bridge here shewn was unfortunately carried away by ice during the winter of 1864. The village is pleasantly situated, but it has suffered from the same causes that have retarded the growth of Lewiston. Near this point the river

QUEENSTON SUSPENSION BRIDGE.

BROCK'S MONUMENT.

becomes more tranquil, the shores appear less broken and wild, and the change in the scenery affords a pleasing transition from the sublime to the beautiful. This Monument stands on the Heights of Queenston, from whence the village derived its name. The present structure occupies the site of the former one, which was blown up, by some miscreant, on the 17th of April, 1840. The whole edifice is one hundred and eighty-five feet high. On the sub-base, which is forty feet square and thirty feet high, are placed four lions, facing north, south, east, and west; the base of the pedestal is twenty-one and a-half feet square, and ten feet high; the pedestal itself is sixteen feet square, ten feet high, surmounted with a heavy cornice ornamented with lion's heads and wreaths, in alto-relievo. In ascending from the top of the pedestal to the top of the base of the shaft, the form changes from square to round. The shaft is a fluted column of freestone, seventy-five feet high and ten feet in diameter, whereon stands a Corinthian capital, ten feet high, on which is wrought, in relief, a statue of the Goddess of War. On this capital is the dome, nine feet high, which is reached by 250 spiral steps from the base, on the inside. On the top of the dome is placed a colossal statue of Gen. Brock.

FORT NIAGARA.

This Fort stands at the mouth of the Niagara River, on the American side. There are many interesting associations connected with this spot; as, during the earlier part of the past century, it was the scene of many severe conflicts between the Whites and the Indians, and subsequently between the English and the French. The names of the heroic La Salle, the courtly De Nouville, and the gallant Prideaux, will long retain a place in the history of this country. The village adjacent to the Fort is called Youngstown, in honor of its founder, the late John Young, Esq.

FORT NIAGARA.

Within the last few years, important repairs have been made around the Fort, and the entire wall has been constructed anew. Here was fought the battle of the 24th July, 1759, in which Prideaux, the English General, fell, and after which the French garrison surrendered to Sir William Johnson, who succeeded to the command of the English.

NIAGARA.

This is one of the oldest towns in Upper Canada, and was formerly the capital of the Province. It is situated where the old town of Newark stood, and is opposite to Youngstown. It faces the river on one side, and Lake Ontario on the other. The trade of this place has been diverted to St. Catherines, since the completion of the Welland Canal; and the other towns upon the Niagara River have suffered in common, from the same cause.

FORT MASSASAUGA.

TORONTO.

Our stay at Niagara having now drawn to a close, we must decide upon the route we shall take for Toronto. There are two means of getting there, one by water and the other by land. On a sunny calm day nothing can be more pleasant than the water excursion, by the fine new steamer "City of Toronto," under command of Capt. D. Milloy, which daily makes two trips each way across Lake Ontario, between Toronto and Lewiston. If this route is decided on, the tourist will have to make for the Suspension Bridge Station, where he will find the cars ready to take him on to Lewiston, a small town on the American shore, almost immediately opposite to Queenston, on the British side, and to which place we have already bent our steps. From Suspension Bridge to Lewiston, the railway follows the course of the river, running along the high ridge overlooking the rapid stream, until we arrive at Lewiston Station. Omnibuses and cabs will be found in attendance to take passengers down to the steamer, which lies about half a mile off. Once embarked, we pass along Niagara River for about ten miles, the current still running very rapidly, until

ALL ROUND ROUTE AND PANORAMIC GUIDE. 41

CITY OF TORONTO, ONT.

it finds its way into Lake Ontario. The first and only stoppage made between Lewiston and Toronto is at the town of Niagara, 16 miles off the Falls. Passengers from the Clifton House can be brought by the cars down to this town without crossing to the American shore, and embark on board the "City of Toronto" here. Almost immediately after leaving Niagara village, we pass between the Two Forts, Niagara and Massasauga, the former garrisoned by American troops, and the latter by the soldiers of Her Majesty Queen Victoria. These two forts are so close together, that it is said, on a calm night, the watchwords as given by the troops on changing guard, can be heard distinctly from one side to the other, across the water. From this point we strike out into the lake, and in the centre almost lose sight of the land behind us before we discern the city of Toronto immediately in front of us. The view of Toronto from the water is very fine indeed, and, judging from the public buildings and wharves, shows it to be a city of some importance and prosperity. Before we commence describing it, however, we must return to Niagara to conduct our tourists who prefer the overland route by the Great Western Railway. They also must make their way to the Suspension Bridge Station, and after leaving they will reach the prettily situated and thriving city of Hamilton, built upon the banks of Lake Ontario, and the head-quarters of the Great Western Railway of Canada, where the general offices, engine sheds and work shops are located. Forty miles more journeying brings the traveller to Toronto in time to catch the Royal Mail Steamer for Montreal, which leaves daily at 2 p.m. We wish, however, to give tourists the opportunity of paying Toronto a visit under our auspices, and acting on our general system, will at once direct them to an hotel where they can be comfortable. The "Queen's Hotel," belonging to Capt. Dick, and the "Rossin House," kept by Mr. Shears, divide between them the share of the visitors' patronage. With either, the tourist will be perfectly satisfied, and though the "Rossin House," which was burnt down a few years back, has been again built and furnished in a sumptuous manner, the "Queen's" has also been lately redecorated and refitted. We shall, therefore, leave our travellers to choose for themselves, with confidence, as at either house they will be well cared for.

Toronto is the chief city of Ontario, or Upper Canada, as the Province used to be called. A large sand bar, of about seven miles in length, terminating at what is called Gibraltar Point, forms, as it were, a well-sheltered and accessible harbor. The former name of this city was Little York, until 1834, when it was changed to Toronto. The streets are well built and broad, and some of the public buildings are remarkably handsome and merit a visit. The University is the chief attraction, and well supports its claim. The style is intended to be pure Norman, though in some of its minor details, modern requirements have made it necessary to depart from it. It stands in a large well-kept park, with avenues of stately trees leading into two of the principal thoroughfares of the city. The massive tower in the centre of the South façade is 120 feet in height. The Normal School and Trinity College on Queen Street West, are both handsome edifices, which will well repay a visit. All these buildings, being devoted to educational purposes, prove Toronto to be second to no other city in the Dominion for the culture of the young. Osgoode Hall, where all the Courts of Law are congregated, is a handsome building enough outside, and inside the arrangements of the different courts, with spacious passages and galleries, are so perfect, that very many cities of more pretensions than Toronto can boast would do well to copy. The Provincial Lunatic Asylum, the Elgin Association for improving the moral and religious condition of the colored population, and the Merchants' Exchange, should all be seen by the visitor. The English Cathedral, dedicated to St. James, and the Roman Catholic Cathedral of St. Michael, deserve notice. There are one or two pretty drives to be made out of the city, though the country around has not much beauty to boast of. The most attractive one, perhaps, is the drive along the road skirting the lake, which, on a fine day, is covered with boats of all shapes and sizes, from the Royal Mail steamers to the miniature skiff with its snow-white sails. As we have said, the Mail Line of boats leave the wharf daily for Montreal. Travellers can go on board, obtain their state-rooms, and make the passage of the Lake; but, as " variety is charming," our tourists can, if they prefer it, go as far as Kingston by the Grand Trunk Railway, and there take the steamer. This is one of the advantages of taking a joint ticket at Niagara Falls, which enables the holder to travel by either rail or boat, and in this way the option of conveyance is with the passenger, giving him the opportunity of consulting his own convenience or inclination, after arrival at Toronto. Tourists arriving from Niagara Falls can have three hours in Toronto, take the evening train and reach Kingston in time to connect with the steamer which left Toronto at 2 p.m. the same day. For a short distance we run along the banks of the Lake and then we lose sight of it altogether. After leaving Toronto the first place

LAKE ONTARIO FROM NIAGARA RIVER.

of any importance we come to is

PORT HOPE,

which is situated sixty-five miles from Toronto. A small stream, which here falls into the Lake, has formed a valley, in which the

LAKE ONTARIO STEAMER.

town is located. The harbor formed at the mouth of this stream is shallow, but safe and commodious. Port Hope is a very pretty town; on the western side, the hills rise gradually one above another. The highest summit, which is called "Fort Orton," affords a fine prospect, and overlooks the country for a great distance around. The village is incorporated, and contains about 2500 inhabitants.

COBOURG

lies seven miles below Port Hope, and contains nearly 5000 inhabitants. The town contains seven churches, two banks, three grist mills, two foundries, and the largest cloth factory in the province It is also the seat of Victoria College and a Theological Institute. Midway between Port Hope and Cobourg is "Duck Island," on which a lighthouse is maintained by the government.

Here the train stops about a quarter of an hour, to give travellers the opportunity of demolishing the very acceptable meal that is ready for them in the Refreshment Room of the Station. A branch line runs up into the backwoods to Peterboro and connects with the Grand Trunk here. The Wesleyans have erected a very handsome building, called Victoria College, and capable of accommodating about 150 students. Cobourg has also a fine town-hall and gaol, two very useful and necessary buildings in their respective ways.

KINGSTON.

This place was call by the Indians, "*Cataracqui.*" A settlement was begun by the French, under De Courcelles, as early as 1672. The Fort, which was finished the next year, was called Fort Frontenac, in honor of the French count of that name. This Fort was

KINGSTON.

ALL ROUND ROUTE AND PANORAMIC GUIDE. 47

CITY OF KINGSTON, ONT.

alternately in the possession of the French and the Indians, until it was destroyed by the expedition under Col. Bradstreet, in 1758. In 1762, the place fell into the hands of the English, from whom it received its present name. Kingston is one of the most important military posts in Canada. It is one hundred and ten miles from Cobourg, and contains about 15,000 inhabitants.

There is a very good Hotel here, " The British American," where Tourists staying on, will find every accommodation and comfort.

[Before proceeding down the St. Lawrence we will retrace our steps and briefly notice the places on the American side of Lake Ontario.]

CHARLOTTESVILLE

is situated at the mouth of the Gennesee River, and is the port of Entry for Rochester. It is seventy-five miles from the mouth of the Niagara. The Geunesee is navigable by steamers to Carthage, five miles from its mouth. At Carthage, passengers can take omnibuses to Rochester, two miles distant.

OSWEGO

is the next port, after passing Charlottesville. It is a beautiful and flourishing town, and contains a population of about 15,000. It is the commercial centre of a fertile and wealthy part of the country, and is the terminus of a railroad and a canal, connecting it with Syracuse and the New York Central Railway. The history of this place is associated with many hard battles, fought during the time of the Indian and the French wars.

CAPE VINCENT RAILROAD DEPOT.

SACKETT'S HARBOR.

This place is situated about forty-five miles from Oswego, and twenty miles from the St. Lawrence. It lies upon the north-eastern shore of Lake Ontario, and derives its name from Mr. Sackett, of Jamaica, L.I., who purchased and took possession of it in 1799. It is admirably fitted, from its position, for a naval station, and is now the seat of a military post, called "Madison Barracks."

THE THOUSAND ISLANDS.

The Royal Mail Steamer, which leaves Toronto on the previous afternoon at 2 o'clock, is due at Kingston between 3 and 4 the following morning. If we go on straight from the train to the steamer, we have a short drive to take from the Railway Station to the wharf, where we shall most probably find the boat ready waiting; and shortly after leaving Kingston we shall be amongst The Thousand Islands, which stretch themselves along the centre of the St. Lawrence for a distance of 40 miles. They are amongst the wonders of the St. Lawrence; situated about six miles below Kingston. There are, in fact, no less than 1800 of these "emerald gems in the ring of the wave," of all sizes, from the islet a few

FORT HENRY—MARTELIO TOWER.
CEDAR ISLAND.

LIGHTHOUSE ON ONE OF THE
THOUSAND ISLANDS.

yards square, to miles in length. It is a famous spot for sporting; myriads of wild fowls of all descriptions may here be found; and angling is rather fatiguing than otherwise, from the great quantity and size of the fish. These islands, too, have been the scene of most exciting romance. From their great number, and the labyrinth-like channels among them, they afforded an admirable retreat for the insurgents in the last Canadian insurrection and for the American sympathizers with them; who, under the questionable name of "patriots," sought only to embarrass the British Government. Among these was one man, who, from his daring and

VIEWS AMONG THE THOUSAND ISLANDS.

ability, became an object of anxious pursuit to the Canadian authorities; and he found a safe asylum in these watery intricacies, through the devotedness and courage of his daughter, whose inimitable management of her canoe was such, that against hosts of pursuers she baffled their efforts at capture, while she supplied him with provisions in these solitary retreats, rowing him from one place of concealment to another, under shadow of the night. But, in truth, all the islands, which are so numerously studded through the whole chain of these magnificent Lakes, abound with materials for romance and poetry. For instance, in the Manitoulin Islands, in Lake Huron, the Indians believe that the *Manitou*, that is, the *Great Spirit* (and hence the name of the islands) has forbidden his children to seek for gold; and they tell you that a certain point where it is reported to exist in large quantities, has never been visited by the disobedient Indian without his canoe being overwhelmed in a tempest.

They firmly believe in this, strange though it may appear, and it is the means of keeping them from attempting to seek for the supposed hidden treasure.

CLAYTON.

This village is situated on the American side, opposite to the "Thousand Islands," and is of considerable importance as a lumber station. Square timber and staves are here made up into large rafts and floated down the St. Lawrence to Montreal and Quebec. These rafts are often very large, and as they require a great number of men to navigate them, the huts erected for their shelter give them, as they pass down the river, the appearance of small villages. Many of the steamers and other craft that navigate Lake Ontario are built here.

ALEXANDRIA BAY

is the next port, after leaving Clayton. It is built upon a massive pile of rocks, and its situation is romantic and highly picturesque. It is a place of resort for sportsmen. Some two or three miles below the village is a position from whence one hundred islands can be seen at one view.

BROCKVILLE.

This village was named in honor of General Brock, who fell on Queenston Heights, in the war of 1812. It is situated on the Canadian side of the St. Lawrence, and is one of the prettiest towns in the province. It is situated at the foot of the Thousand Islands, on an elevation of land which rises from the river in a succession of ridges. The town was laid out in 1802, and is now a place of considerable importance. The present population is about 5,500. Those who wish to stay here a few days for fishing or shooting will find themselves very comfortable at "Campbell's Hotel."

OGDENSBURGH

is situated on the American side of the river. In the year 1748, the Abbé François Piquet, who was afterwards styled the "Apostle of the Iroquois," was sent to establish a mission at this place, as many of the Indians of that tribe had manifested a desire of embracing Christianity. A settlement was began in connection with this mission, and a fort, called "La Presentation," was built at the mouth of the Oswegatchie, on the west side. The remains of the walls of this Fort are still to be seen. In October, 1749, it was attacked by a band of Indians from the Mohawks, who, although bravely repulsed, succeeded in destroying the pallisades of the fort and two of the vessels belonging to the colony. The Abbé Piquet retired from the settlement soon after the defeat of Montcalm, and finally returned to France, where he died in 1781. Ogdensburgh has increased rapidly within the past few years, and will doubtless become a large manufacturing place. The Northern Railroad, (now leased by the Vermont Central Company) which runs to Lake Champlain, a distance of one hundred and eighteen miles, and which connects at Rouse's Point with the railroads to Boston and Montreal, has its terminus here. The Northern Transportation Company's Steamers connect here with the Northern Railroad.

PRESCOTT

is situated on the Canada side of the St. Lawrence, opposite Ogdensburgh, and contains over 3000 inhabitants. About a

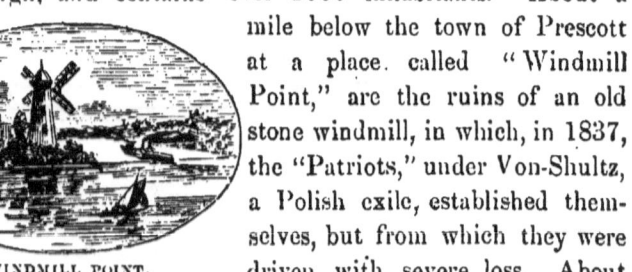
WINDMILL POINT.

mile below the town of Prescott at a place called "Windmill Point," are the ruins of an old stone windmill, in which, in 1837, the "Patriots," under Von-Shultz, a Polish exile, established themselves, but from which they were driven with severe loss. About five miles below Prescott is Chimney Island, on which the remains of an old French fortification are to be seen. The first rapid of the St. Lawrence is at this island.

At Prescott, those intending to visit Ottawa will leave the boat. This city, the Capital of the Dominion, is only a little more than fifty miles distant from Prescott, and the journey to it can easily be performed by railway in about three hours. We can confidently recommend this detour, on account of the claims of Ottawa itself, of which more anon. Passengers wishing to make this trip can obtain return tickets at moderate fares, and join the steamer at Prescott the following morning and descend the Rapids to Montreal, which is by far the most exciting portion of the whole journey.

Having disembarked from our boat, we cross the wharf to the St. Lawrence and Ottawa Railway Company's Station, where we find cars waiting to take us on to the Capital of the Dominion,

OTTAWA.

After a journey of about two hours and a-half over the 54 miles of the St. Lawrence and Ottawa Railway we shall be landed at the very unpretentious station of the Capital, at about five o'clock, p.m. Our steps will naturally be directed towards the "Russell House," under the management of Mr. J. A. Gouin. Here accommodation is provided for over 250 guests, and every comfort afforded at a reasonable charge, the whole arrangements being carried on under the personal supervision of Mr. Gouin, who will see that his visitors, during their stay under his roof, want for nothing. Ottawa (or Bytown as it used to be called) has been selected by Her Majesty as the new Capital of the Dominion, the chief seat of Government having for many previous years been settled at the cities of Montreal, Quebec and Toronto, in turns, for a certain number of years at each. This system was found to work very badly, and numerous quarrels arose between all of these cities, and the jealousy stirred up against the one that happened at the time to be favoured made it necessary to choose some fourth place, and Ottawa was selected as being the most central and desirable that could be found. The Government buildings have consequently been erected here, and very much credit is due not only to the architect who has designed these most beautiful

PARLIAMENT BUILDINGS, OTTAWA.

buildings, but to the public spirit of the Legislature who have found the means for bringing the work to a successful termination. The Parliament Buildings with the Departmental offices, and the Queen's Printing House, occupy three sides of a square, on a bluff of ground overlooking the river, called Barrack Hill.

They contain two Legislative Halls, one for the Senate, the other for the House of Commons, both being the same size as these provided in the English Houses of Parliament for the Lords and Commons, and, like their originals, very handsomely decorated and conveniently furnished. A large Library is also provided, capable of accommodating half a million volumes. The buildings are designed in the Italian-Gothic style, and constructed of stone found in the neighborhood. When it is stated that the cost was $2,500,000, and the position almost unique, the tourist ought not to lose the opportunity of going there, as they alone are quite worth the few days' delay which must necessarily be devoted to the sight. The rest of the city, which is of course much increasing, and the whole of it nearly new, is very handsomely and substantially built. Sparkes street, the scene of the assassination of the late Hon. T. D'Arcy McGee, is close to the Parliamentary Buildings and the Russell House. Like Quebec, Ottawa is divided into an Upper and a Lower town, the link between the two being the substantially built bridge spanning the Rideau Canal, which here falls into the Ottawa after passing through eight stone locks. This canal connects the Ottawa River with Kingston and Lake Ontario, through a series of lakes and streams, running in its entire length about 135 miles. The other chief attractions in the neighborhood of Ottawa are the Chaudière Falls, considered by very many to rank next in importance, beauty and grandeur to Niagara. They stand, or rather fall, immediately above the city, at its western extremity, the width of the greater fall being two hundred feet, while its depth is forty—the boiling, seething, foaming character of the water giving name to the place. On the northern side is the smaller, or Little Chaudière, and here the waters, after their leap, seem to go into some subterranean passage, by which they are carried off until they appear again at a place called "The Kettles," half-a-mile lower down. Of course, the existence of such passages is a mere matter of conjecture, which we will leave to the study of Geologists, and others interested, to determine. Before leaving Ottawa, we ought to pay a visit to one of the Timber Slides, which are tolerably frequent in the upper river. One is erected on the northern bank, and we will here tarry for a moment whilst we watch the fate of one of those huge rafts of hewn wood down its headlong rush. These water-shoots are erected for the purpose of getting the fallen trees from the higher level down to the river, at the smallest possible cost, and wherever water can be obtained in sufficient quantity this has been done. Where the descent is very steep, these "shoots" are broken up at stated intervals into long straight runs, in order to destroy the impetus which the raft would naturally acquire. The descent on one of the rafts down the timber slide is a thing only to be attempted by those who possess bold and steady nerves. To say that there is much danger in such an excursion would be to over-exaggerate the risk, whilst to say that there is none, would be as far from the truth. An application to the "boss" of a gang of raftsmen would, without difficulty, obtain the privilege of a ride down.

THE OTTAWA RIVER TO MONTREAL.

Tourists desiring to go by this route can leave by steamboat, which starts daily, Sundays excepted, at 6.30 a.m. At this hour, and no later, the "Queen Victoria," one of the very handsome steamers of the Ottawa River Navigation Company, commanded by Captain Bowie, starts from her wharf, between the picturesque and thickly-wooded banks of the Ottawa River. Soon after leaving we obtain a fine view of the Rideau Falls, which make their descent on the south side into the river. The drapery or curtainlike drop has given it its name, and gracefully and gently as it falls over, it resembles more a sheet of thin glass than a waterfall. About a mile and a-half below Ottawa, the river Gatineau, one of the longest and most important tributaries of the Ottawa, flows into the river. Shortly after leaving Ottawa, breakfast is announced in the handsome saloon of the boat, and 18 miles off our starting point, we stop at Buckingham. Thurso, a flourishing little village, doing a large and satisfactory trade in lumber, is our next stopping point, and after two hours' more steaming, through really lovely country, and with two more stoppages at villages called Brown's and Major's, we reach L'Orignal, and here we wish our travellers to leave the boat, for the purpose of visiting the Caledonia Springs, nine miles off, postponing the rest of the trip to Montreal until the following day's steamer arrives, to take them on their way once again. The medicinal and healing qualities of these Springs, of which there are four in number, are very well established, and during the summer months, people flock here in large numbers to partake of the waters and to enjoy one another's society. A splendid new hotel of solid masonry, and capable of accommodating two hundred guests, has been lately erected. Bowling alleys and billiard rooms have been fitted up, and the baths increased in number quite lately, and supplied with every convenience.

Having rejoined our boat on the following day at L'Orignal, or proceeded in it without having made the proposed excursion to the Springs, as the case may be, we come, after seven miles, to Grenville, where we have to disembark and take a twelve miles' ride on the Railway cars to Carillon. The reason for this is, that at Grenville rapids commence and continue for the distance named, and as they are not navigable for steamers, it would take up too much time for the boats to go through the Locks of the Canal. Opposite Grenville, and at the commencement of the first (Long Sault) rapids, stands Hawkesbury, where some very large saw mills, belonging to the Hon. John Hamilton, have been erected. It is computed that at these mills alone, 30,000,000 feet of timber are annually cut and sawn. At Carillon, we find the " Prince of Wales," (a sister ship to the one we have lately left,) under the command of Capt. Shepherd, waiting to take us on to Lachine. Before quitting this spot, we may remark that the Boundary line between the former provinces of Upper and Lower Canada, now respectively known by the names of Ontario and Quebec, leaves the centre of the river here (which had been the division for many hundred miles), and branches off in a direct line for the St. Lawrence. The banks of the river about here are high and thickly wooded, whilst its width varies between half and a quarter of a mile. On the southern shore the MOUNTAIN OF RIGAUD stands out conspicuously against the sky, but as dinner is announced about the time we are approaching the village of the same name, we will not say much more about it for fear of spoiling the tourist's appetite, by drawing him away from the well-arranged meal waiting his digestion in the saloon. The small village of POINTE-AUX-ANGLAIS is reached at 2 p.m., HUDSON, (where there are some extensive glass works), at 2.30, and COMO, at 2.45, and here the river expands from about half-a-mile wide into a lake of about eight miles. This is called the LAKE OF TWO MOUNTAINS, after the two mountains to be seen on the north side rising four to five hundred feet from the water. The highest of these hills is called CALVARY, and held sacred by the tribes of the Indians inhabiting the small village of OKA, the place we see on our left hand standing at the junction between the lake and the river, and where our steamer stops for the last time before crossing the Lake to St. Anne's. The Iroquois and Algonquins live in this village together, a stone wall running between the two tribes and dividing the village into two, whilst the Roman Catholic Church acts as the bond of union between them. Immediately in front of us we see the Island of Montreal, one branch of the river passing round the Island by the right (which we follow), and the other going round to the left, and henceforth known as the Back River. Three quarters of an hour more and we are passing through the Canal and Lock at St. Anne's, in order to avoid the small rapids which run to our right under the bridge belonging to, and crossed over by, the Grand Trunk Railway. This Bridge, although on a much smaller scale than the Victoria Bridge at Montreal, is an exceedingly fine structure and must not be overlooked. St. Anne's has been immortalized by Moore, in his famous Canadian Boat Song, and which is believed to have been written in the pretty little village itself. Many people know the first two lines of the chorus—Row, brothers, row, &c.,—and no more, so we fancy it will not be out of place to reproduce it here in its short entirety:—

"Faintly as tolls the evening chime
    Our voices keep tune, and our oars keep time.
    Soon as the woods on shore look dim,
    We'll sing at St. Anne's our parting hymn.
        Row, brothers, row, the stream runs fast,
        The Rapids are near and the daylight's past.

"Why should we yet our sail unfurl?
    There is not a breath the blue wave to curl;
    But when the wind blows from off the shore,
    Oh! sweetly we'll rest our weary oar.
        Blow, breezes, blow, the stream runs fast,
        The Rapids are near and the daylight's past.

"Uttawas' tide! this trembling moon
    Shall see us float o'er thy surges soon.
    Saint of this green isle! hear our prayers,
    Oh, grant us cool heavens and favoring airs.
        Blow, breezes, blow, the stream runs fast,
        The Rapids are near and the daylight's past.

During the summer months St. Anne's is visited by large numbers of families from Montreal, its nearness to the city making it easy of daily access for business men, whilst the charming opportunities it offers for fishing and aquatics renders it very justly sought after by the angler and amateur sailor. A mile below St. Anne's, we get into Lake St. Louis, where the Ottawa and St. Lawrence unite for the first time. As this part of our journey will also be reviewed by us when conducting our travellers from Prescott to Montreal direct, we will simply say that the "Prince of Wales" is due to arrive at Lachine at 4.20 p.m., and that the cars of the Champlain section of the Grand Trunk Railway will be in waiting to take her passengers direct to Montreal, which place they will reach about 5 p.m.

THE RIVER ST. LAWRENCE TO MONTREAL.

Returning to our steamer, which we left at Prescott, after discharging her travellers for Ottawa. &c., we must continue our course down the St. Lawrence to Montreal, congratulating ourselves that it has been found not only possible but perfectly safe to take these large steamers through the rapids (which commence within a few miles of Prescott), instead of necessitating the constant change from boat to stage coach, and stage coach back again to boat, as many as from five to six times between Prescott and Montreal, as our ancestors and forefathers had to do less than twenty-five years ago.

The next town on the American side is Waddington; and in the river, over against it, is Ogden Island. On the Canada side is Morrisburg, formerly called West Williamsburg. It is called the Port of Morristown, and contains about two hundred inhabitants.

GALLOPS RAPIDS.   CHRYSLER'S FARM.

A short distance below Morristown, on the Canada side, is Chrysler's Farm, where, in 1813, a battle was fought between the English and the Americans. The Americans were commanded by General Wilkinson, and were at that time descending the river to attack Montreal. The attempt was afterwards abandoned. Thirty miles below Ogdensburg is Louisville, from whence stages run to Massena Springs, distant seven miles.

LONG SAULT.

This is a continuous rapid of nine miles, divided in the centre by an island. The usual passage for steamers is on the south side. The channel on the north side was formerly considered unsafe and dangerous; but examinations have been made, and it is now descended with safety. The passage in the southern channel is very narrow, and such is the velocity of the current that a raft, it is said, will drift the nine miles in forty minutes.

DESCENT OF THE RAPIDS.

This is the most exciting part of the whole passage of the St. Lawrence. The rapids of the "Long Sault" rush along at the rate of something like twenty miles an hour. When the vessel enters within their influence the steam is shut off and she is carried onwards by the force of the stream alone. The surging waters present all the angry appearance of the ocean in

LONG SAULT RAPIDS.

a storm ; the noble boat strains and labors : but, unlike the ordinary pitching and tossing at sea, this going down hill by water produces a highly novel sensation, and is, in fact, a service of some danger, the imminence of which is enhanced to the imagination by the tremendous roar of the headlong, boiling current. Great nerve, and force, and precision are here required in piloting, so as to keep the vessel's head straight with

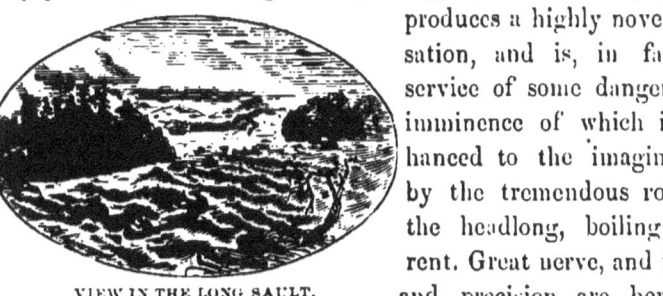

VIEW IN THE LONG SAULT.

62 ALL ROUND ROUTE AND PANORAMIC GUIDE.

STEAMERS DESCENDING LOST CHANNEL LONG SAULT RAPIDS.

ALL ROUND ROUTE AND PANORAMIC GUIDE. 63

the course of the rapid; for if she diverged in the least, presenting her side to the current, or "broached to," as the nautical phrase

BATISTE, AN INDIAN PILOT, STEERING A STEAMER DOWN THE RAPIDS
OF THE ST. LAWRENCE.

is, she would be instantly capsized and submerged. Hence the necessity for enormous power over her rudder; and for this purpose the mode of steering affords great facility, for the wheel that governs the rudder is placed ahead, and by means of chain and pulley sways it. But in descending the rapids a tiller is placed astern to the rudder itself, so that the tiller can be manned as well as the wheel. Some idea may be entertained of the peril of descending a rapid, when it requires four men at the wheel and two at the tiller to ensure safe steering. Here is the region of the daring raftsmen, at whose hands are demanded infinite courage and skill; and, despite of both, loss of life frequently occurs.

RAFT DESCENDING THE RAPIDS.

ST. LAWRENCE CANALS.

	Miles.	Locks.	L. Ft.
Gallops Canal,	2	2	8.
Point Iroquois Canal,	3	1	6.
Rapid Platt Canal,	4	2	11.6
Farren's Point Canal,	¾	1	4.
Cornwall Canal, Long Sault,	11½	7	48.
Beauharnois Canal, Coteau,			
Cedars, Split Rock, Cascade Rapids,	11¼	9	82.6
La Chine Canal, La Chine Rapids,	8½	5	44.9
Fall on portions of the St. Lawrence between canals from Lake Ontario to Montreal,			17.
From Montreal to tide water at Three Rivers,			12.9
	41	27	234.½

The St. Lawrence canal was designed for paddle steamers, but from the magnitude of the rapids and their regular inclination, the aid of the locks is not required in descending the river. Large steamers, with passengers, leave the foot of Lake Ontario in the

ALL ROUND ROUTE AND PANORAMIC GUIDE. 65

STEAMER DESCENDING ONE OF THE RAPIDS OF THE ST. LAWRENCE.

E

morning, and reach the wharves at Montreal by daylight, without passing through a single Lock.

ENTRANCE TO CORNWALL CANAL.

DICKINSON'S LANDING.

CORNWALL.

This is a pleasant town, situated at the foot of the Long Sault, on the Canada side. Here vessels are passed up the river by the Cornwall canal, and come out into the river about twelve miles above. The boundary line between the United States and Canada passes near this village, and the course of the St. Lawrence is hereafter within Her Majesty's dominions.

ST. REGIS

is an old Indian village, and lies a little below Cornwall, on the opposite side of the river. It contains a Catholic church, which was built about the year 1700. While the building was in progress, the Indians were told by their priest that a bell was indispensable in their house of worship, and they were ordered to collect furs sufficient to purchase one. The furs were collected, the money was sent to France, and the bell was bought and shipped for Canada; but the vessel which contained it was captured by an English cruiser, and taken into Salem, Massachusetts. The bell was afterwards purchased for the church at Deerfield.

ST. REGIS INDIANS.

The priest of St. Regis, having heard of its destination, excited the Indians to a general crusade for its recovery. They joined the expedition fitted out by the governor against the New England colonists, and proceeded through the then long, trackless wilderness, to Deerfield, which they attacked in the night. The inhabitants, unsuspicious of danger, were aroused from sleep only to meet the tomahawk and scalping-knife of the savages. Forty-seven were killed, and one hundred and twelve taken captive; among whom were Mr. Williams, the pastor, and his family. Mrs. Williams being at the time feeble, and not able to travel with her husband and family, was killed by the Indians. Mr. Williams and a part of his surviving family afterwards returned to Deerfield, but the others remained with the Indians, and became connected with the tribe. The Rev. Eleazár Williams, one of the supposed descendants from this family, has been mysteriously identified with the lost Dauphin of France. The Indians, after having completed their work of destruction, fastened the bell to a long pole, and carried it upon their shoulders, a distance of nearly one hundred and fifty miles, to the place where Burlington now stands; they buried it there, and in the following spring removed it to the church at St. Regis, where it now hangs.

LAKE ST. FRANCIS.

This is the name of that expansion of the St. Lawrence which begins near Cornwall and St. Regis, and extends to Coteau du Lac, a distance of forty miles. The surface of this lake is interspersed with a great number of small islands. The village of Lancaster is situated on the northern side, about midway, of this lake.

COTEAU DU LAC

is a small village, situated at the foot of Lake St. Francis. The name, as well as the style of the buildings, denotes its French origin. Just below the village are the Coteau Rapids.

CEDARS.

This village presents the same marks of French origin as Coteau du Lac. In the expedition of Gen. Amherst, a detachment of three hundred men, that were sent to attack Montreal, were lost in the rapids near this place. The passage through these rapids is very exciting. There is a peculiar motion of the vessel, which in descending seems like settling down, as she glides from one ledge to another. In passing the rapids of the Split Rock, a person unacquainted with the navigation of these rapids will almost involuntarily hold his breath until this ledge of rocks, which is distinctly seen from the deck of the steamer, is passed. At one time the vessel seems to be running directly upon it, and you feel certain that she will strike; but a skilful hand is at the helm, and in an instant more it is passed in safety.

CEDAR RAPIDS.

BEAUHARNOIS

is a small village at the foot of the Cascades, on the south bank of the river. Here vessels enter the Beauharnois canal, and pass around the rapids of the Cascades, Cedars, and Coteau, into lake St. Francis, a distance of fourteen miles. On the north bank, a branch of the Ottawa enters into the St. Lawrence. The river again widens into a lake called the St. Louis. From this place a view is had of Montreal Mountain, nearly thirty miles distant. In this lake is Nun's Island, which is beautifully cultivated, and belongs to the

CASCADES FROM ENTRANCE TO
BEAUHARNOIS CANAL.

RAPIDS NEAR "THE CEDARS"—RIVER ST. LAWRENCE.

NUN'S ISLAND

Grey Nunnery, at Montreal. There are many islands in the vicinity of Montreal belonging to the different nunneries, and from which they derive large revenues.

LA CHINE.

This village is nine miles from Moutreal, with which it is connected by railroad. The La Chine Rapids begin just below the town. The current is here so swift and wild that to avoid it a canal has been cut around these rapids. This canal is a stupendous work, and reflects much credit upon the energy and enterprise of the people of Montreal.

CAUGHNAWAGA.

This is an Indian village lying on the south bank of the river, near the entrance of the La Chine Rapids. It derived its name from the Indians that had been converted by the Jesuits, who were called "*Caughnawagas,*" or " praying Indians." This was probably a misnomer, for they were distinguished for their predatory incursions upon their neighbors in the

CAUGHNAWAGA VIILLAGE.

New England provinces. The bell that now hangs in their church was " the proceeds" of one of these excursions.

No one should come to Montreal without "shooting the Rapids, and to those who reach it by train, or from the Ottawa River, it is quite easy for them to enjoy the excitement; for every morning at 7 o'clock a train leaves Bonaventure Station for Lachine, connecting with the beautiful little steamer "Aurora," which starts from the Railway Wharf as soon as she has her freight of travellers, shoots the rapids, passes under the Victoria Bridge, and lands her passengers again in Montreal by nine in the morning, with an appetite for breakfast much heightened by their early excursion. But to return to our steamer. After leaving Caghnawaga and having run the rapids, we pass the village of La Prairie, and immediately come in sight of the city of Montreal, commercially and actually the most important place in British North America, and destined some day, perchance, to rival the population and the prosperity of some of the overgrown cities of the Old World.

Before reaching the wharf, we pass under the centre span of the eighth wonder of the world — the Victoria Bridge of the Grand Trunk Railway of Canada.

MONTREAL,

the largest and most populous city, in fact the commercial metropolis of British North America, is pleasantly situated upon the south shore of an island; and at the base of Mount Royal, from which both the city and the island take their name. Its population is about 130,000. The island is about thirty miles long, and ten broad, and is formed by the River Ottawa debouching into the St. Lawrence, at its western and eastern extremities, the former near St. Annes, the latter at Bout de l'Isle. It is famed for the fertility of its soil.

The city was founded in 1642, upon its present site, and for a long time bore the name of *Ville Marie*. Hochelaga was the name of the original Indian village, upon which a portion of the city is built, and the eastern suburb of it still retains the name. It was first explored by Jacques Cartier in 1535. Of its early history

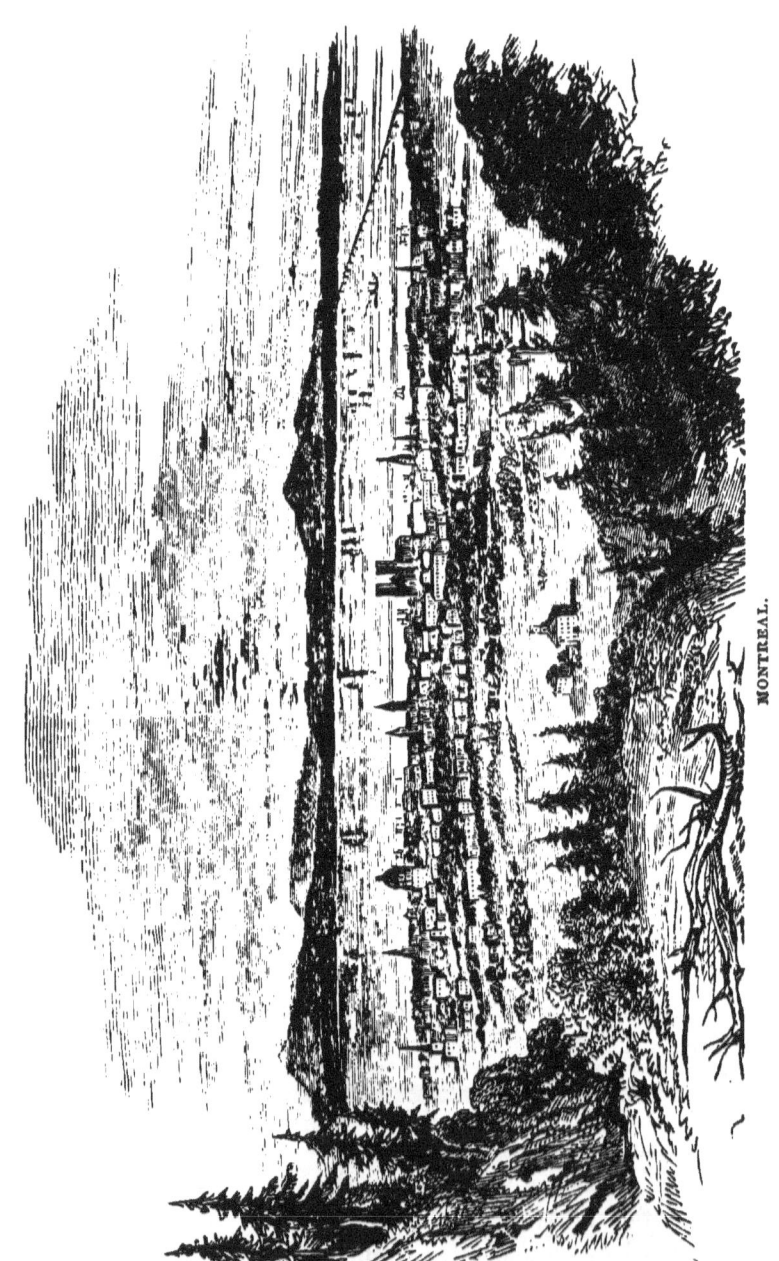
MONTREAL.

nothing has come down to us beyond that the French settlers were constantly annoyed by the ravages of the Iroquois Indians. In 1758 it had a population of about 4000 souls, and had evidently been laid out upon the old French plan of narrow streets, and was divided, as now, into upper and lower town; the upper part then being the level of the present Court House. According to an old chronicle : " In the lower town the merchants and men of business chiefly resided, and here also were the place of arms, the royal magazines, and the Nunnery Hospital. The principal buildings were in the upper town, such as the palace of the Governor, the houses of the chief officers, the Convent of the Recollets, the Jesuits' Church and Seminary, the Free School, and the Parish Church. The houses were solidly constructed in that semi-monastic style peculiar to Rouen, Caen, and other towns in Normandy : some of the buildings of that period are still standing. It was for a long time the head-quarters of the French forces in Canada. In 1763 it was surrendered to the English, and about that time it was described as a city of an oblong form, surrounded by a wall flanked with eleven redoubts, a ditch about eight feet deep, and of a proportionable width, but dry, and a fort and citadel.

At the beginning of the present century vessels of more than 300 tons could not ascend to Montreal, and its foreign trade was carried on by small brigs and barques. In 1809 the first steam vessel, called The Accomodation, built by the Hon. John Molson, made a trip to Quebec; she had berths for about twenty passengers. Now, behold the contrast that fifty years of industry, intelligence, enterprise and labor have produced — ocean steamers of 3000 tons ; the magnificent steamers of the Richelieu Company, vieing in splendor and comfort with the far famed Hudson River boats; ships, from 700 to 1200 tons, from all parts of the world, lying alongside the wharves of the harbor—which are not equalled on this continent, in point of extent, accommodation, approach and cleanliness.

The city, as seen from its approach by steamboat, with Mount Royal for a background, covered with beautiful villas, interspersed.

here and there with tall spires, is majestic, and for beauty almost unrivalled.

The river frontage is nearly three miles in length, extending from the Victoria Bridge to the village of Hochelaga. For upwards of a mile it has an excellent stone retaining wall from the entrance to the Lachine Canal to below the Bonsecours Market, which, with its glittering dome, forms one of the most conspicuous objects in the right foreground, and contrasts with the neighboring spire of the Bonsecours Church, one of the oldest churches in Montreal. We scarcely think the view from the steamer can be paralleled as you pass under the centre tube of the Victoria Bridge, and first view the long array of glittering spires, the lofty towers of the Parish Church of Notre Dame, the well proportioned tower of the Royal Insurance Buildings, and the long unbroken line of cut stone stores flanking the wharf.

LIVERPOOL AND MONTREAL SCREW STEAMER.

We will now suppose the stranger landed at the base of Jacques Cartier Square : the first thing arresting his eye will be the Bonsecours Market and Town Hall; it is an imposing building of a quasi-Doric character, surrounded with a large dome ; it is divided into three storeys, the basement and first floor serving the purpose of a market, which is always supplied with an excellent stock of provisions. The upper part is occupied by the various city offices, and by the city concert hall—a room capable of containing four thousand persons. The building cost about £75,000.

ALL ROUND ROUTE AND PANORAMIC GUIDE. 75

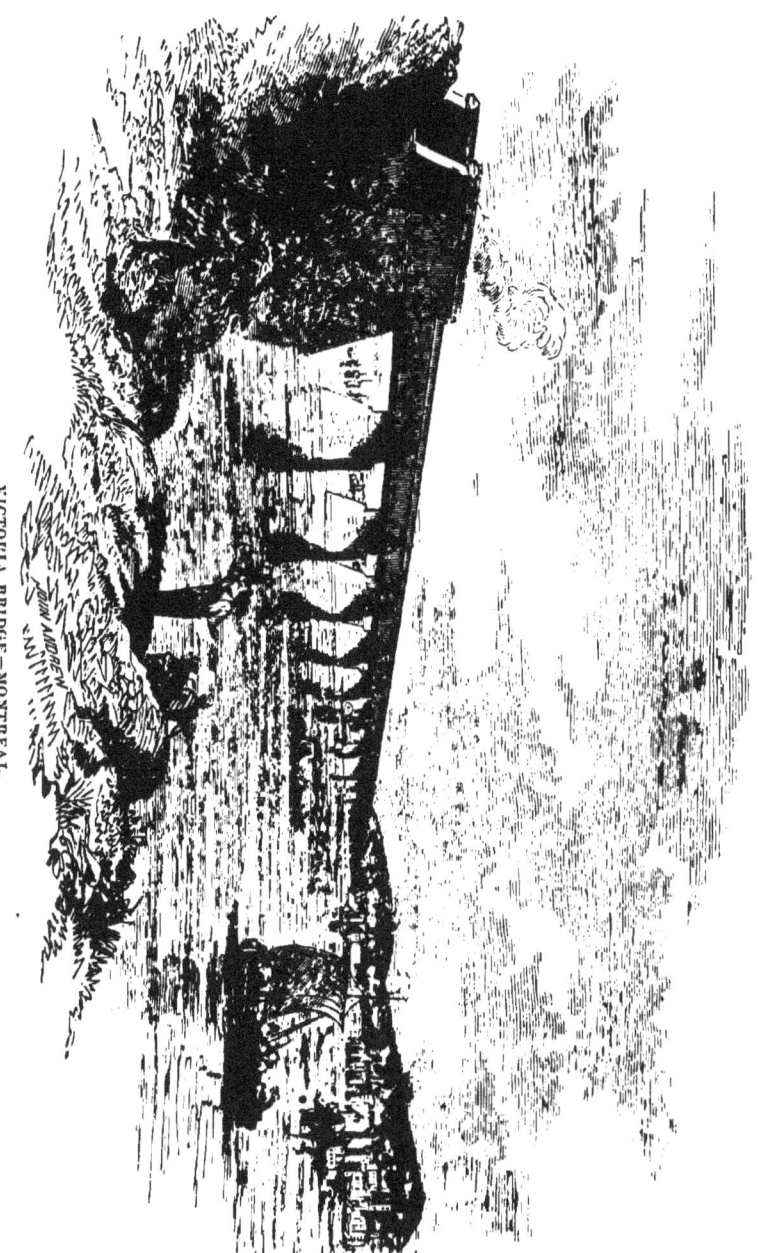

VICTORIA BRIDGE—MONTREAL.

Proceeding through Jacques Cartier Square he need not pause to examine Nelson's monument, but can turn to the left and view the Court House, an Ionic structure, about a hundred and twenty feet long by about seventy in height; it contains all the judiciary courts, as well as the Prothonotary's office and Court of Bankruptcy. There is a very valuable law library, containing upwards of 6,000 volumes. At the back of the Court House is the Champ de Mars, a well kept parade ground, upon which the different regiments in garrison, and the Volunteer Militia parade; upon it three thousand troops may be manœuvred. During the summer some one or other of the regiments of the line, or the volunteers, are exercised.

Going from the Court House, on the road to the St. Lawrence or Ottawa hotels, the visitor enters a square called Place d'Armes. It is not large in dimensions, but few on this continent, if any, can equal it in point of its buildings. On the left is the Cathedral of Notre Dame, said to be the largest in North America, and capable of holding ten thousand people. It is about 260 feet long, by 140 feet broad, and the front facing the square is flanked by two massive towers 220 feet in height. In the one on the left there is a peal of bells, one of which goes by the name of "Gros Bourdon." It is said to weigh nearly 30,000 lbs.; it has a deep base sound, and is used as a fire alarm. The tower on the right can be ascended upon the payment of a small fee, and from its battlement a most wonderful prospect is obtained—the broad rolling waters of the St. Lawrence, nearly two miles wide, lying almost at the feet of the spectator, covered with shipping; to the right the Victoria Bridge, Nun's Island, the village of Laprairie, with the glittering steeple, the boiling rapids of Lachine, the blue hills of Vermont in the far off distance—to the left, the beautiful island of St. Helen's, covered with trees clothed in the proud prosperity of leaves, the villages of St. Lambert and Longueuil, and the river studded with islands, until its silver course is lost at the village of Verchères.

On the side of the square facing the Cathedral are the Montreal and City Banks. The former one of the most imposing public buildings in the city; it is built of cut limestone; its style, modern Grecian. On the left hand of the square are the Merchants' Bank, Ontario Bank, the London and Liverpool Insurance Company's office. The former is built of Ohio sandstone; the style is Italian; the proportions are good. This row is a pretty piece of street architecture. On the right hand side is a fine block called Muir's buildings, a very imposing edifice. The fourth is occupied by the honorable fraternity of Freemasons, holding under the Canadian Register. The lodge room is 52 feet long by 34 wide, and is 16 feet high. There are several anterooms. The interior of the lodge room is well furnished and decorated. Next to this block is the British and American Express offices, and the Cosmopolitan Hotel, kept by Gianelli. The centre of the square is laid out as a garden, with a fine fountain.

Adjoining the square is Great St. James-street, in which there are some fine buildings—

The Post-office, a well proportioned building, and very conveniently arranged. Opposite to it is the far famed hostelry, the St. Lawrence Hall. It has been under the skilful management of Mr. Hogan, the proprietor, for the last seventeen years, and has been gaining in public favor every succeeding year. It is capable of putting up 500 visitors, and during the months of travel this accommodation is nightly required, so much so, that visitors are frequently unable to obtain rooms. Passing down this side of the street the first building that arrests the attention is the Methodist church, a very commodious and well arranged interior; it possesses one of the finest organs in the city. Just below is Nordheimer's Hall—the basement is occupied by Messrs. Gould and Hill, music instrument sellers. On the first floor is a music hall, capable of holding a thousand people, now used as a billiard hall. At the end of the street is a large block occupied by the firm of Henry Morgan & Co., dry goods merchants; it occupies the site of the old American Presbyterian church, built in 1825-6. Nearly opposite this is the Ottawa Hotel, a very fine house capable of accommodating 300 persons, and now kept by Mr. Burnett. Passing on is a novel store front, the premises of Messrs. Prowse; it is highly ornamental and composed of zinc. Next is Molson's Bank, the most pretentious building in Montreal; it has two frontages or façades faced with Ohio sandstone. The shafts of the Doric columns of the portico and those of the Corinthian columns on the Great St. James-street front are of polished Peterhead granite.

Turning down Peter-street, past Molsons Bank, upon the left, is a very handsome block, " Caverhill's Buildings "—these stores, without exception, are not surpassed by anything in British North America. They are six stories in height, cut limestone. The front is an elaborate composition in the Italian Palazzo style, bold and massive in character. At the bottom of Peter-street runs right and left St. Paul-street, wherein are congregated nearly all the principal dry goods and hardware stores. This street is a credit to the modern enterprise of Montreal. It is symbolic of the wealth of the city.

St. Patrick's Hall, in Victoria-square, has been lately finished. It stands alone, and contains one of the finest halls in America, extending the entire length and breadth of the building on the upper floor, 134 feet by 94 feet, and 46 feet high. The lower storeys are devoted to library, committee rooms, a billiard hall, and stores. It is built of Montreal limestone, the style of architecture being an adaptation of the Norman. The Albert Buildings, in Victoria-square, and the Dominion Block, in McGill-street, are quite lately erected, in the best style possible for wholesale stores and offices, and are most imposing buildings, quite surpassing anything previously attempted in the Dominion. Opposite to the Dominion Buildings is situated the Albion Hotel, well known amongst travellers, and kept by Messrs. Decker & Co.

It will now be simply a duty to point out the various places and things in the city or vicinity of Montreal worth seeing.

Foremost is the Geological Museum, facing the Champ de Mars, in Gabriel-street; this is an institution that Canada may well be proud of. It is under the direction of that able geologist, Sir Wm. Logan; this science has never had one connected with it whose soul was more in his work, and whose ability was better able to direct the geological survey of so great a mineral country as Canada.

The University of McGill College, with its museum, and that of the Natural History Society, near the English Cathedral, are well worthy of inspection. The tourist can gain information relative to the zoology and ornithology of Canada; and to those who are disciples of Isaac Walton, the curator of the Natural History Society can give any information regarding the fishing grounds.

It has been remarked, "let me see the resting place of the dead and I will form an estimate of the living." Granting the premises, we can say, go to the Mount Royal Cemetery. It will compare favorably with the far-famed Père la Chaise at Paris. The cemetery is passed in what is called " the drive round the two mountains"; this is a favorite pastime with the inhabitants of Montreal, and a very delightful drive it is; going by St. Lawrence-street, there is a fine country from Côte des Neiges across the island to the " Back River" or Ottawa, with its numerous hamlets, convents and churches; and for a pic-nic commend us to the *Priests' Island*, close to the old mill by the rapids, Sault au Recollet, a delightful spot, and where, during the season, a good day's fishing is to be had.

MONTREAL AND VICTORIA BRIDGE.

The Victoria Bridge ought to be visited; visitors are allowed to examine the first tube without an order, and as they are all alike to see one tube is to see all. The Bridge is a wonderful structure, and reflects as much credit on the successful builders as upon the original designers. The bridge proper rests upon twenty-four piers, and is about a mile and a quarter long. The piers are all at a distance of 242 feet, with the exception of the two centre piers; these are 330 feet; upon these rest the centre tube, which is 60 feet above the summer level of the St. Lawrence. The piers, or at least their abutments, present to the down stream, which is about seven miles per hour, a sharp-pointed edge, to resist the pressure of the ice in the winter, which offers a resistance of many thousands of tons; the piers are calculated to resist a pressure of seventy thousand tons. At the centre of the bridge is an opening, from this there is a magnificent view of the river. The important part this bridge plays with the uninterrupted communication of the Western traffic with that of the United States—Boston, Portland, &c.—need not be dilated on. It is more than commensurate with its cost— which was nearly 7,000,000 dollars. It gives to Montreal an unbroken railway communication of 1,400 miles.

The English Cathedral (Episcopal), in St. Catherine-street, is by far the most perfect specimen of Gothic architecture in America. It is well worthy a visit. The whole neighborhood is studded with churches — Roman Catholic, Presbyterian, Wesleyan and Methodist—each vieing with a lofty spire to make the ecclesistical architecture of the city worthy of comparison with the many public buildings with which Montreal abounds.

The new church of the Jesuits is a very imposing edifice. The interior is covered with frescoes of some incident in the lives of our Saviour and His Apostles.

Erskine church, and John Knox church, (Scotch Presbyterian), are two fair specimens of modern Gothic. The Wesleyan Church, with its graceful lantern and spire, forms a conspicuous object, though its dimensions are overtopped by the large American Presbyterian church adjoining it.

A little further westward is a pretty little Gothic church (Episcopalian), dedicated to St. James the Apostle; and beyond that again, in the large Roman Catholic Seminary, at the Priest's farm, is a beautiful chapel, well worthy inspection. The grounds and gardens attached to the seminary are the most beautiful in Canada.

WATER WORKS.—The water is taken from the St. Lawrence about one and a-half miles above the Lachine Rapids, where the elevation of the river surface is about 37 feet above the Harbour of Montreal. The Wheel house at the termination of the aqueduct is worthy of notice. The water is admitted to and discharged from this building through submerged archways under covered frost proof passages, extending above and below the building. There are two iron wheels 20 feet diameter and 20 feet broad. These wheels are upon the suspension principle, " high breast" or " pitch back," with ventilated buckets. These reservoirs are excavated out of the solid rock, and have a water surface of over ninety thousand square feet, 206 feet above the harbour, with a depth of 25 feet. The length is 623 feet, with a breadth of 173, formed into two reservoirs by a division wall. The two contain about fifteen million gallons. Total cost of aqueduct, machinery, pumping-main, and reservoirs about $1,800,000.

Fire Alarm Telegraph was recently erected, and proved a thorough success. The chief office is in the City Hall, from which it has connections with upwards of 64 boxes, the church bells, several public clocks, the Observatory and Water Works near McGill College.

A favourite trip is that to Belœil Mountain, near St. Hilaire. The latter is a station on the Grand Trunk Railway, about 18 miles from Montreal, and where several trains stop during the day, so that that there will be no difficulty in performing the trip without remaining at the village for the night. From St. Hilaire Station, the tourist proceeds to the pretty little village of Belœil, and when conducted to the base of the mountain, it can be ascended with comparative ease—even by ladies—by a circuitous path, passing through a maple grove, which leads to a beautiful lake, formed in the hollow of the mountain. This lake abounds with fish. This is the general resting place, before the ascent to the peak, upon the summit of which used to be a small oratory, surmounted with a huge cross covered with bright tin; this cross was visible upwards of thirty miles. From the site of the oratory, about 1,500 feet above

82   ALL ROUND ROUTE AND PANORAMIC GUIDE.

the level of the River St. Lawrence, can be obtained a panoramic view, sixty miles in radius.

From Montreal, we propose to take our travellers down the river to Quebec, and, as we have now mentioned the chief points to be seen in this interesting city, we will prepare for our departure.

The Richelieu Company own two splendid vessels, the "Montreal" and the "Quebec," which make the trip between Montreal and Quebec every night, except Sunday, during the time that navigation is open. Any traveller preferring the land route, can take the trains leaving Bonaventure Station on the Grand Trunk Rail-

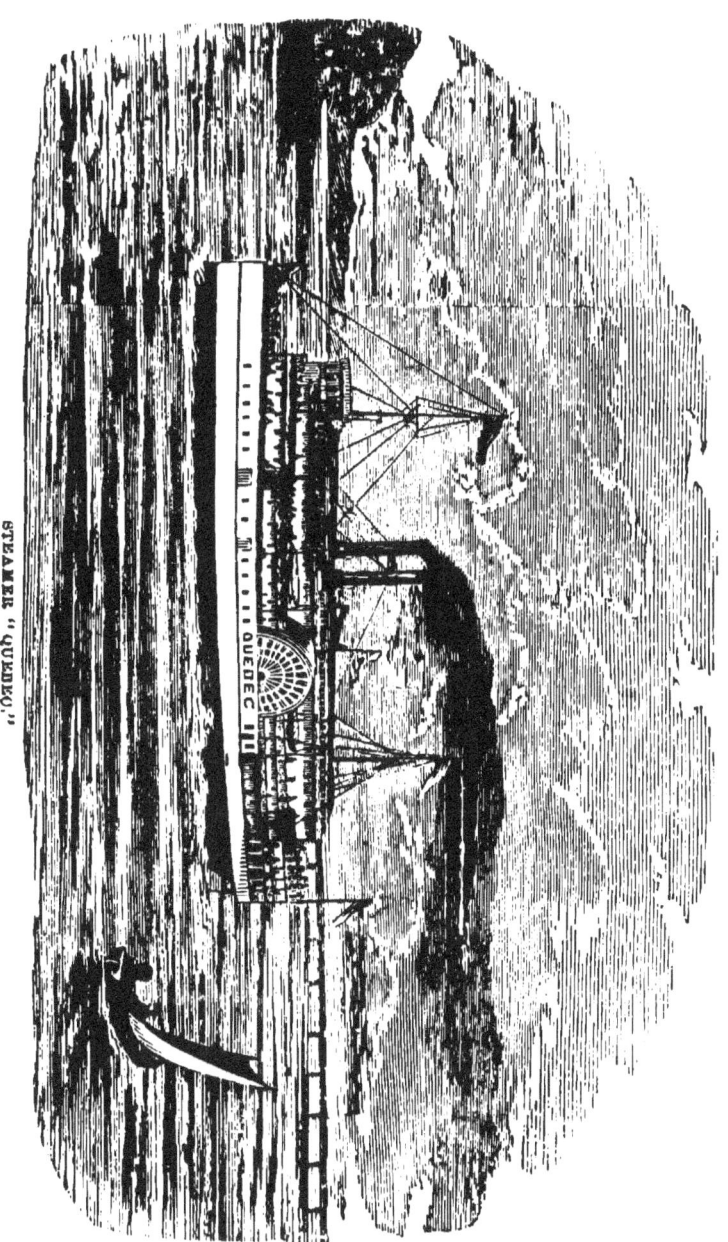

STEAMER "QUEBEC."

way, and, after an eight hours' journey, be deposited at Point
Levi, opposite "the Ancient Capital," as Quebecers are fond of
styling their city, whence a steam ferry will soon land them across
the river. To our mind, however, the most agreeable route is to
go on board the "Quebec," take a stateroom, and be landed early
next morning at one of the quays of Quebec.

LONGUEUIL

is a small village on the south bank of the river, three miles below
Montreal.

WILLIAM HENRY,

or Sorel, is situated at the junction of the Richelieu, the outlet of
Lake Champlain with the St. Lawrence. It is forty-five miles
below Montreal, and is the first stopping-place for steamers on their
way to Quebec. The town is laid out in the form of a quadrangle,
and contains a number of good buildings, the principal of which
are the Roman Catholic and the English churches. The population is over 3000.

LAKE ST. PETER

is an expansion of the St. Lawrence, beginning about five miles
below Sorel, and extending in length twenty-five miles; its greatest
breadth is nine miles. It is quite shallow, except in a narrow
channel, which is navigable for ocean steamers and sailing vessels
of very large tonnage coming up to Montreal during the summer
season. There are several islands at its western extremity. Port
St. Francis is a small village, situated on the south shore of Lake
St. Peter, eighty-two miles below Montreal. It is a place of but
little importance.

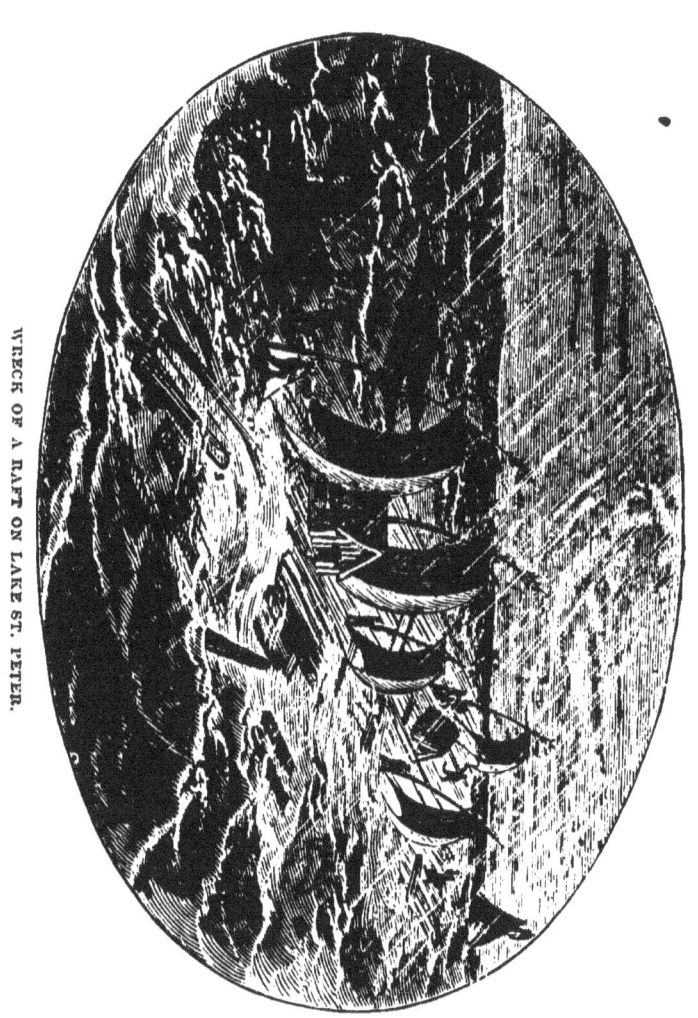

WRECK OF A RAFT ON LAKE ST. PETER.

THREE RIVERS

is situated at the confluence of the rivers St. Maurice and St. Lawrence, ninety miles below Montreal, and the same distance above Quebec. It is one of the oldest settled towns in Canada, having been founded in 1618. It is well laid out, and contains many good buildings, among which are the Court House, the Gaol,

ROMAN CATHOLIC PARISH CHURCH.　　　　NUNS.

the Roman Catholic Church, the Ursuline Convent and the English and the Wesleyan Churches. The population of Three Rivers is over 6000.

BATISCAN

is situated on the north shore of the river, one hundred and seventeen miles below Montreal. It is the last place at which the steamers stop before reaching Quebec. It is a place of little importance.

In passing down the St. Lawrence from Montreal, the country upon its banks presents a sameness in its general scenery, until we approach the vicinity of Quebec. The villages and hamlets are decidedly *French* in character, and are generally made up of small buildings, the better class of which are painted white or whitewashed, with red roofs. Prominent in the distance appear the tile-covered

CANADIAN HABITANTS.

spires of the Catholic Churches, which are all constructed in that unique style of archi'ecture so peculiar to that church.

CANADIAN FARMHOUSE.

The rafts of timber afford a highly interesting feature on the river as the traveller passes along. On each a shed is built for the raftsmen, some of whom rig out their huge, unwieldy craft with gay

CANADIAN PRIEST.

CANADIAN PEASANT.

CANADIAN BOATMEN.

streamers, which flutter from the tops of poles. Thus, when several of these rafts are grappled together, forming, as it were, a floating island of timber half a mile wide and a mile long, the sight is extremely picturesque; and when the voices of these hardy sons of the forest and the stream join in some of their Canadian boat songs, the wild music, borne by the breeze along the water, has a charming effect. Myriads of these rafts may be seen lying in the coves at Quebec, ready to be shipped to the different parts of the world.

QUEBEC.

As soon as the traveller is landed, we recommend him to make his way as quickly as possible to either the "St. Louis Hotel" or "Russell House," both of which establishments are kept by Messrs. Russell & Sons, who honestly deserve to be classed amongst the most enterprising hotel proprietors on the American continent. At either of these houses the tourist will find himself at home and well cared for, surrounded by every comfort he can possibly desire The "St. Louis" has been very much enlarged and improved, to meet the increasing requirements of the American travel, and too much credit cannot be awarded to the Messrs. Russell, who are ever ready to embark their means for the purpose of inducing their friends from the States to pay the old Capital a visit. Every modern convenience and luxury is to be found in these hotels, and we are quite satisfied that the experience of any one who may visit Quebec will be like our own, and lead to oft repeated journeys to the old City.

Quebec, until recently the capital of United Canada, is situated on the north shore of the St. Lawrence, in lat. 46 deg. 48 min. north, and long. 71 deg. 15 min. west, from Greenwich. It was founded by Charlevoix, in 1608, on the site of an Indian village, called *Stadacona*. It is the second City in British America, and has a population of more than 50,000. The form of the city is nearly that of a triangle, the Plains of Abraham forming the base, and the rivers St. Lawrence and St. Charles the sides. It is divided into two parts, known as the Upper and the Lower Towns. The Upper Town is strongly fortified, and includes within its limits the Citadel of Cape Diamond, which is known to be the most formidable fortress in America. The Lower Town is built upon a narrow strip of land which runs at the base of the cape and of the high ground upon which the Upper Town stands, and the suburbs of St. Roch's and St. John's extend along the river St. Charles and to the Plains of Abraham. Quebec was taken by the British and colonial forces in 1629, but restored to France in 1632; and was finally captured by Wolfe in 1759, and, together with all the French possessions in North America, was ceded to Great Britain at the peace of 1763.

Quebec, including the city and suburbs, contains 174 streets; among the principal of which are the following :—*St. John's-street*, which extends from Fabrique-street to St. John's-gate, in the Upper Town, and is occupied chiefly by retail stores; *St. Louis-street* a handsome and well built street, extending from the Place d'Armes to the St. Louis-gate, and occupied principally by lawyers' offices and private dwellings; *D'Autueil-street* faces the Esplanade and the ground where the artillery are drilled, and

CITY OF QUEBEC.

is an elegant street, mostly of private dwellings; *Grand Allée*, or *St. Louis-road*, outside St. Louis-gate, and leading to the Plains of Abraham, is a pleasant and beautiful street, on which are many elegant villa residences; *St. John-street*, without, is also a fine street, occupied by shops and private dwellings. The principal street in the Lower Town is *St. Peter* on which, and on the wharves and small streets which branch from it, most of the banks, insurance companies, and merchant's offices are situated.

Durham Terrace, in the Upper Town, is a platform commanding a splendid view of the river and the Lower Town. It occupies the site of the old castle of St. Louis, which was burnt in 1834, and was erected by the nobleman whose name it bears.

The Public Garden fronts on Des Carrières-street, Upper Town, and contains an elegant monument, which was erected to the memory of Wolfe and Montcalm, in 1827. The height of this monument is 65 feet; its design is chaste and beautiful, and no stranger should leave Quebec without visiting it.

The Place d'Armes is an open piece of ground, around which the old château of St. Louis, the government offices, the English cathedral, and the Court House are situated.

The Esplanade is a beautiful piece of ground, situated between D'Auteuil-street and the ramparts.

The Citadel, on Cape Diamond, is one of the most interesting objects to visitors; and those who are desirous of seeing it should make application to the town major, at the main guard-house, from whom tickets of admission can always be obtained by persons of respectability. The area embraced within the fortifications of the citadel is more than forty acres.

The line of fortifications, enclosing the citadel and the Upper Town, is nearly three miles in length, and the guns with which they are mounted are mostly thirty-two and forty-eight pounders. There are five gates to the city, three of which, Prescott, Palace and Hope gates, communicate with the Lower Town, and two of which, St. Louis and St. John's-gate, communicate with the suburbs of the same name. About three quarters of a mile from the city are four Martello Towers, fronting the Plains of Abraham, and intended to impede the advance of an enemy from that direction.

The Roman Catholic Cathedral, which fronts upon the Upper Town market-place, is a large and commodious building, but with no great pretensions to architecture. The interior is handsomely fitted up, and has several fine paintings by the old masters, which are well worthy of inspection. The church will seat 4,000 persons. It has a good organ.

St. Patrick's Church, on St. Helen-street, Upper Town, is a neat and comfortable building, and is capable of seating about 3,000 persons.

St. Roch's Church, on St. Joseph and Church-streets, in the St. Roch's suburbs, is a large and commodious building, and will seat 4,000 persons. There are several good paintings in this church.

The Church of Notre Dame des Victoires, on Notre Dame-street, is one of the oldest buildings in the city. It has no pretensions to architectural beauty, but it is comfortably fitted up, and will seat over 2,000 persons.

PROTESTANT CHURCHES.

The English Cathedral is situated between Garden-street, St. Ann-street, and the Place d'Armes, Upper Town, and is a handsome edifice, 135 by 75 feet, and will seat between 3,000 and 4,000 persons. This church, which was erected in 1804, has a good organ, and is neatly fitted up in the interior.

Trinity Church, situated on St. Nicholas-street, Upper Town, is a neat cut stone building, erected in 1824. It is 74 by 48 feet, and the interior is handsomely fitted up.

St. Peter's Chapel is situated on St. Vallier-street, St. Roch's, and is a neat plain structure, which will seat about 500 persons.

St. Paul's, or *The Mariner's Chapel*, is a small building near Diamond Harbor, designed principally for seamen.

St. Andrew's Church, in connection with the Church of Scotland, is situated on St. Ann-street, Upper Town. The interior is well fitted up, and will seat over 1,200 persons.

St. John's Free Scotch Church, is situated on St. Francis-street, Upper Town. It is a neat plain structure, and will seat about 600 persons.

The Wesleyan Chapel, on St. Stanislaus-street, is a handsome Gothic building, erected in 1850. The interior is well fitted up, and it has a good organ. It will seat over 1,000 persons.

The Wesleyan Centenary Chapel is situated on D'Artigny-street, and is a plain but substantial edifice.

The Congregational Church, on Palace-street, Upper Town, is a neat building of cut stone, erected in 1841, and will seat about 800 persons.

The Baptist Church, on St. Ann-street, Upper Town, is a neat stone building, and will seat over 400 persons.

The other principal public buildings worthy of notice are :—

The Hotel Dieu, hospital and church, which front on Palace-street, Upper Town, and, connected with the cemetery and garden, cover an area of about ten acres. The buildings are spacious and substantial, and the hospital has beds for about sixty sick persons.

The General Hospital is situated on the river St. Charles, in the St. Roch's ward. The hospital, convent, and church are a handsome quadrangular pile of stone buildings, well adapted to the purpose for which they are designed.

The Ursuline Convent, situated on Garden-street, Upper Town, was founded in 1641. A number of fine paintings are to be seen here, and application for admission should be made to the Lady Superior.

The University of Quebec fronts on Hope-street and the marketplace, Upper Town. The buildings, which are of massive gray stone, form three sides of a quadrangle, and have a fine garden in the rear.

The Court House and the *City Hall* are substantial stone buildings, situated on St. Louis-street, and well adapted to their respective purposes.

The Gaol is situated at the corner of St. Ann and St. Stanislaus-streets, Upper Town, and is a massive stone building, and cost about £60,000. It is in a healthy location, and well adapted to the purpose for which it was designed.

The Jesuit Barracks front on the Upper Town market-place and St. Ann-street. They have accommodations for about 1,000 men.

The Marine Hospital, situated on the river St. Charles, in the St. Roch's ward, is intended for the use of sailors and emigrants, and is a beautiful stone building of four storeys. It was erected at a cost of £15,000, and will accommodate about 400 patients.

The Lunatic Asylum is situated at Beauport, two and a-half miles from Quebec, and is an extensive building, enclosed in a park of about 200 acres.

The Quebec Music Hall is a handsome cut stone edifice, recently erected, situated on St. Louis-street, Upper Town.

As the Seat of French Power in America until 1759, the great fortress of English Rule in British America, and the key of the St. Lawrence, Quebec must ever possess interest of no ordinary character for well informed tourists. Living is comparatively cheap, and Hotel accommodation equal to Montreal in every respect.

The City and environs are rich in drives, in addition to being on the direct line of travel to the Saguenay, Murray Bay, Cacouna, Rimouski, Gaspé and other noted watering places.

A City, crowning the summit of a lofty cape, must necessarily be difficult of access; and when it is remembered how irregular is the *plateau* on which it stands, having yet for thoroughfares the identical Indian paths of Stadacona or the narrow avenues and approaches of its first settlers in 1604, it would be vain to hope for regularity, breadth and beauty in streets, such as modern cities can glory in. It is yet in its leading features a City of the 17th century—a quaint, curious, drowsy, but healthy location for human beings; a cheap place of abode; if you like a crenelated fort with loop-holes, grim-looking old guns, sentries, pyramids of shot and shell; such is the spectacle high up in the skies, in the airy locality called the Upper Town. Some hundred feet below it appears a crowded mart of commerce, with vast beaches, where rafts of timber innumerable rest in safety, a few feet from where a whole fleet of *Great Easterns* might float secure on the waters of the famed river. The two main roads outside the City, the St. Foy and St. Louis-roads, are lined by the country seats of successful Quebec merchants, judges, professional men, retired English officers, &c., &c.

On his way from the St. Louis Hotel, St. Louis-street, the tourist notices, a few steps to the west, the antiquated one storey house where Brigadier General Richard Montgomery was laid out after being found in his snowy shroud at Pres-de-Ville, 31st December, 1775. After passing the Drill Shed, the Military Home, the Ladies Protestant Home, facing St. Bridget's Home, and adjoining the area which the Quebec Seminary intend to lay out as a Botanical Garden, the Jehu, amidst most miraculous details of the great battle, soon lands his passenger on the Plains of Abraham, close to the little monument which marks the spot where James Wolfe, the British hero expired, near to the well from which water was procured to moisten his parched lips. A few minutes more brings one to Mr. Price's Villa, Wolffield, where may be seen the rugged path up the St. Denis burn, by which the Highlanders and English soldiers gained a footing above, on the 13th September, 1759 ;—destined to revolutionize the new world— the British, guided by a French prisoner of war, brought with them from England (Denis de Vitré, an old Quebecer,) or possibly by Major Stobo, who had, in 1758, escaped from a French prison in Quebec and returned to his countrymen, the English, accompanying Saunders' fleet to Quebec. The tourist next drives past Thornhill, Sir Francis Hinck's old home, when Premier to Lord Elgin. Opposite appears the leafy glades of Spencer Wood, so grateful a summer retreat that my lord used to say, "There he not only loved to live, but would like to rest his bones." Next comes Spencer Grange, then Woodfield, the beautiful homestead of the Hon. Wm. Sheppard in 1840, and of the late Jas. Gibb for many years after. The eye next dwells on the little rustic chapel of St. Michael, embowered in evergreens; then villas innumerable are seen, that is, if you enter beyond the secluded portals of *Sous-les-Bois*—Benmore, Col. Rhodes' country seat, Clermont, Beauvoir, Kilmarnock, Cataraqui, Kelgraston, Kirk-Ella, Meadow Bank, &c., until after a nine miles' drive, Redclyffe closes the rural landscape. Redclyffe is on the top of the cape of Cap Rouge, where many indications yet mark the spot where Roberval's ephemeral colony wintered as far back as 1541. The visitor can now return to the city by the same road, or select the St. Foy-road, skirting the classic heights where General Murray, six months after the first battle of the Plains, lost the second, on 28th April, 1760—the St. Foy Church was then occupied by the British soldiers. Next comes Holland's House, Montgomery's headquarters in 1775, behind which is "Holland Tree," overshadowing, as of yore, the graves of the Hollands.

The view of the meandering St. Charles below, especially during the high tides, is something to be remembered. The tourist shortly after detects the iron pillar, surmounted by a bronze statue of Bellona, presented in 1855 by Prince Napoleon Bonaparte, intended to commemorate this fierce struggle.

In close proximity appears the bright *parterres* or umbrageous groves of *Bellevue*, Hamwood, Bijou, Westfield and *Sans Bruit*, the dark gothic arches of Finlay Asylum, and the traveller re-enters by St. John Suburbs, with the broad basin of the St. Charles and the pretty Island of Orleans staring him in the face.

Drive down next to see Montmorency Falls, and the little room which the Duke of Kent, Queen Victoria's father, occupied in 1791. A trip to the Island of Orleans in the ferry will also repay trouble : it costs very little; half an hour of brisk steaming will do it, cross then to St. Joseph, Levi, per ferry steamer, and go and behold the most complete, the most formidable, as to plan the most modern, earth works in the world. Drive to Lake Beauport, to luxuriate on its red trout; but mind you stop on your return and take a caulker of Glenlivet or old Bourbon or Sillery Mousseux on the banks of the trout stream, next to the Hermitage, at Charlesbourg. Step in the *Château;* sit down, like Volney amidst the ruins of Palmyra, and meditate on the romantic though unhappy fate of dark-eyed Caroline, Bigot's Rosemond,* some hundred years ago. You imagine you have seen everything; not so, my friend! tell your driver to let you out opposite Ringfield, on the Charlesbourg-road, and if at home Mr. G. H. Parke, the obliging proprietor, will surely grant you leave to visit the extensive earthworks behind his residence, raised by Montcalm in 1759—so appropriately called Ringfield; hurry back to town in time to accept *that* invitation to dine at the Club, then spend the evening agreeably at the Morrin College, in the cosy rooms of the Literary and Historical Society, and retire early, preparing yourself for the great compaign of the morrow.

TO THE LAKES! TO THE LAKES!

Here are a few of them : Lake Calvaire, at St. Augustin; Lake St. Joseph, Lake *à la Truite*, Lake Philippe, *Lac Jaune*, Snow Lake, *Lac Blanc, Lac Sud-ouest, Lac Vincent, Lac Thomas, Lac Claire*, Lake Mackenzie, Lake Sagamite, Lake Burns, Lake Bonnet,—all within a few hours drive from Quebec, with the exception of Snow Lake. It is not uncommon to catch trout weighing from 12 lbs. to 20 lbs. in Lake St. Joseph and Snow Lake during the winter months.

* You will peruse Caroline's pathetic tale in that repository of Canadian lore, Maple Leaves, which you will find a trusty guide for objects without the City, whilst Hawkins' Historical Picture of Quebec will, in language most classic, enlighten you as to what Quebec contains or did contain within its old walls.

We feel sure our reader, whatever his pretensions may be as a traveller, will be delighted with the ancient City of Quebec, and have a satisfactory feeling of pleasure within himself for having included it in the catalogue of places he has put down as worthy of a visit in his tour through Canada. The scenery outside the City, and all along the river on both shores, is exceedingly picturesque, every yard bringing a new and varied landscape into view, calculated to please the imagination, delight the eye, and satisfy the most fastidious in natural beauty.

We find the following in Buckingham's Canada : " The situa-
" tion of Quebec is highly advantageous in a commercial as well as
" military point of view ; and its appearance is very imposing
" from whatever quarter it is first approached. Though at a
" distance of 400 miles from the sea, the magnificent river on
" which it is seated is three miles in breadth a little below the
" town, and narrows into about a mile in breadth immediately
" abreast of the Citadel, having in both these parts sufficient
" depth of water for the largest ships in the world—a rise and fall
" of twenty feet in its tides—and space enough in its capacious
" basin, between Cape Diamond on the one hand, and the Isle of
" Orleans on the other, to afford room and anchorage for a
" thousand sail of vessels at a time, sheltered from all winds, and
" perfectly secure."

THE FALLS OF MONTMORENCI.

In taking our departure from Quebec, and on our way down the river, we pass this celebrated cascade. These falls, which are situated in a beautiful nook of the river, are higher than those of Niagara, being more than two hundred and fifty feet; but they are very narrow—being only some fifty feet wide. This place is a very celebrated focus of winter amusements. During the frost, the spray from the falls accumulates to such an extent as to form a cone of some eighty feet high. There is also a second cone of inferior altitude, called the " Ladies' Cone," and it is this of which visitors

ALL ROUND ROUTE AND PANORAMIC GUIDE. 99

FALLS OF MONTMORENCI.

make the most use, as being less dangerous than the higher one. They carry "toboggins,"—long, thin pieces of wood,—and having arrived at the summit, place themselves on these and slide down with immense velocity. Ladies and gentlemen both enter with equal spirit into this amusement. It requires much skill to avoid accidents, and sometimes people do tumble head over heels to the bottom. Visitors generally drive to this spot in sleighs, taking their wine and provisions with them; and upon the pure white cloth which nature has spread out for them, they partake of their dainty repast, and enjoy a most agreeable pic-nic. One does not feel in the least cold, as the exercise so thoroughly warms and invigorates the system. There are men and boys in attendance for the purpose of bringing down strangers who may desire to venture down the icy mountain, and to those who enjoy this kind of pleasure, it is great sport. The drive to the Falls is very beautiful; the scenery on the road through Beauport, where the Provincial Lunatic Asylum is built, and back again being full of interest. The distance of these falls from Quebec is eight miles. About two miles above the Falls is a curious formation on the river bank, called "the Natural Steps," being a series of layers of the limestone rock, each about a foot in thickness, and for about half-a-mile receding one above the other, to the height of nearly 20 feet, as regularly as if formed by the hand of man. They are a great object of wonder and curiosity, and, being so near the Falls, should certainly be included in the visit.

THE CHAUDIERE FALLS,

on the river Chaudière, nine miles below Quebec, are also a favorite resort, and are very beautiful and romantic. The river here is about four hundred feet wide, and the height of the falls is one hundred and thirty feet.

THE LOWER ST. LAWRENCE RIVER.

Leaving Quebec, we advise the tourist to at once make his arrangements for visiting that very popular resort, the Saguenay. For the past few years, thousands of Canadians and Americans have wended their way to this famous River, and the result of their experience has been to make it still more popular. None who have been have resolved otherwise than to repeat the trip the first time they could possibly do so, and to those who have not enjoyed this most lovely of all excursions, we would say, in the language of Shakspeare, " stand not upon the order of your going, but go at once." All information concerning the means of transit can be ascertained at the hotels to which we took our *compagnons de voyage;* but in case they may neglect to attend to the important duty of seeking such requisite knowledge, we would say that during the season two steamers run between Quebec and the Saguenay. Both these boats belong to the Canadian Navigation Company, whose steamers ply between Hamilton, Toronto and Montreal. They are elegantly fitted up for the comfort of passengers, and furnished with every convenience; indeed, there is nothing wanting to render the journey down the river what it always is, most delightful. Once on board and off, we find ourselves steaming away down stream at a good speed, and to turn our thoughts away from the city we have just left, we come in sight of

THE ISLAND OF ORLEANS,

situated in the river St. Lawrence, immediately below Quebec, nineteen miles long by five and a half miles wide, and, like the Island of Montreal, superior in fertility to the main land adjacent to it. Its present population is about six thousand.

THE FALLS OF ST. ANNE

are situated on the river of the same name, on the north side of the St. Lawrence, twenty-four miles below Quebec, and present a variety of wild and beautiful scenery, both in themselves and their immediate neighborhood.

LAKE ST. CHARLES,

thirteen miles north of Quebec, is a favorite resort for tourists, particularly for those who are fond of angling, as the lake abounds in fine trout.

GROSSE ISLE

is situated thirty miles below Quebec. Here is the Quarantine Station,—a sorrowful place everywhere; but there is an unusually melancholy interest attached to this one, from the fact that no less than six thousand Irish emigrants were buried in one grave during the terrible year of famine in Ireland. Apart from these saddening recollections, the island is a fair and agreeable spot, and its scenery is very beautiful. Below this island the river becomes wider and wider, and we soon lose sight of land altogether.

MALBAIE,

90 miles below Quebec, is the first stopping place for the steamer after leaving Quebec, and where many may desire to go ashore and spend a day or two before going further. Murray Bay (Malbaie) is a great resort in the summer months, and many Canadian families spend the entire season in this healthy retreat. Every one must enjoy a few days passed at this fashionable watering place. Leaving it and steaming across the river, which is about 20 miles wide at this point, we strike Rivière du Loup, situated on the south shore. Here those desirous of visiting the far-famed watering-place of Cacouna, can, after an exceedingly pleasant drive through the country of about 6 miles, find themselves in a fashionable place, containing some very good buildings. The "St. Lawrence Hall," where we advise the visitor to make for, is a

large house, replete with every modern convenience and comfort; every accommodation to be obtained at any of our first city hotels can be found there, together with a good Billiard Room, Bowling Alley, and hot and cold baths; sea-bathing is provided for in connection with the hotel, and sailing boats are kept ready for the

CACOUNA BAY.

use of visitors desirous of going out on the river on fishing and shooting excursions. A week spent with "mine host" at the St. Lawrence will always be looked back to with pleasure.

Leaving the wharf at Rivière du Loup, our steamer points her course again to the opposite shore, and in less than two hours we find ourselves at Tadousac, which is at the mouth of the River Saguenay. This is a very pleasant spot, and, if no more time can be spared than the brief stay of the steamboat at the wharf, let us advise the tourist to immediately go ashore. There is a fine hotel here which is excellently kept, and in connection with it are all kinds of sports for the amusement of visitors. The bathing at this place is also very superior. It is a post of the Hudson's Bay Company, who have a considerable establishment here.

Getting aboard again, the whistle is sounded, and we are under steam, and are really now entering the justly-renowned River

TADOUSAC.

Saguenay, and commence, as if by instinct, to strain our eyes and open our mouths, to feast on and swallow all the magnificent natural grandeur that bursts upon us.

THE SAGUENAY RIVER.

The Saguenay is the largest tributary of the great St. Lawrence, and unquestionably one of the most remarkable rivers on the Continent. It is the principal outlet of Lake St. John, which is its head-water: a lake about forty miles long, surrounded by a heavily timbered and level country; its waters are remarkably clear, and abound in a great variety of fine fish. Eleven large rivers fall into it, yet it has only this one outlet; into the lake there is a remarkable curtain fall of two hundred and thirty-six feet, so conspicuous as to be seen at forty or fifty miles distant, the Indian name for which is "Oucat Chouan" or "Do you see a fall there?" The Lake lies about 150 miles north-east of the St. Lawrence, and nearly due north of Quebec. The original name of the Saguenay was Chicoutimi, signifying "Deep water;" but the early Jesuit missionaries gave it the name it now bears, said to be a corruption of St. Jean Nez. The scenery is wild and romantic in the highest degree. The first half of its course averages half-a-mile in width and runs through an almost untrodden wilderness; it abounds in falls and rapids, and is only navigable for the Indian canoe. A few miles below the southern fall in the river is the village of Chicoutimi, at the junction of a river of the same name, which is the outlet of a long lake named Kenokami, with the Saguenay. Here is a range of rapids which extend ten miles. The Indians say there is a subterranean fall above the foot of the rapids, which they call "Manitou," or the "Great Spirit." To avoid these falls there is a carrying place called "Le Grande Portage." An extensive lumber business is transacted here; the village has an ancient appearance, and contains about five hundred inhabitants. The only curiosity is a rude Catholic Church, said to have been one of the earliest founded by the Jesuits. It occupies the centre of a grassy lawn, surrounded by shrubbery, backed by a cluster of wood-crowned hills, and commands a fine prospect, not only of the Saguenay, but also of the spacious bay formed by the confluence of the two rivers. In the belfry of this venerable church hangs a clear-toned bell, with an inscription upon it which has never yet been translated or expounded. From ten to twelve miles south of Chicoutimi, a beautiful expanse of water, called Grand or Ha! Ha! Bay, recedes from the Saguenay, to the distance of several miles.

The village of Grand Bay, 132 miles from Quebec, is the usual resort for those who wish to remain any time in the neighborhood of the Saguenay. The name Ha! Ha! is said to be derived from the surprise which the French experienced when they first entered it, supposing it to be still the river, until their shallop grounded on the north-western shore. At the northern head of it is another settlement, called Baggotville. Between these two places the Saguenay is rather shallow (when compared with the remainder of its course) and varies in width from two and a-half to three miles. The tide is observable as far north as Chicoutimi, and this entire section of the river is navigable for ships of the largest class, which ascend thus far for lumber.

That portion of the Saguenay extending from Ha! Ha! Bay to the St. Lawrence, a distance of nearly sixty miles, is chiefly distinguished, and properly so, for its wonderful scenery. The shores are composed principally of granite, and every bend presents to view an imposing bluff—many of these tower perpendicularly into the air, and seem ready to totter and fall at any moment—it appears awful, in steaming up the Saguenay, to raise the eyes heavenward and behold, hanging directly over head, a mass of granite weighing, perhaps, nearly a million tons. Here, as at Niagara, we feel the insignificance of man as we gaze upon the Almighty's handiworks.

Descending from Ha! Ha! Bay, a perpendicular rock, nine hundred feet high, is the abrupt termination of a lofty plateau called The Tableau, a column of dark-colored granite, 600 feet high by 300 wide, with its sides as smooth as if they had received the polishing stroke from a sculptor's chisel. Statue Point is also another gem of scenery; but the great attractions in the Saguenay are Cape Eternity and Trinity Point, on the south shore, six miles above St. John's Bay. If the only recompense for a visit to the Saguenay was a sight of these stupendous promontories, we are quite sure no visitor would ever regret it. There is an awful grandeur and sublimity about them, which is perfectly indescribable. The steamers shut off steam at these points, and the best view possible is arranged for the passengers by the Captain. The water is said to be as deep five feet from their base as it is in the centre of the stream, and, from actual measurement, many portions of it have been ascertained to be a thousand feet, and the shallowest parts not less than a hundred; and from the overhanging cliffs it assumes a black and ink-like appearance. Cape Eternity is by far the most imposing, and an Indian hunter, having followed a Moose to the brow of the cliff after the deer had made a fatal spring far down into the deep water, is said to have lost his

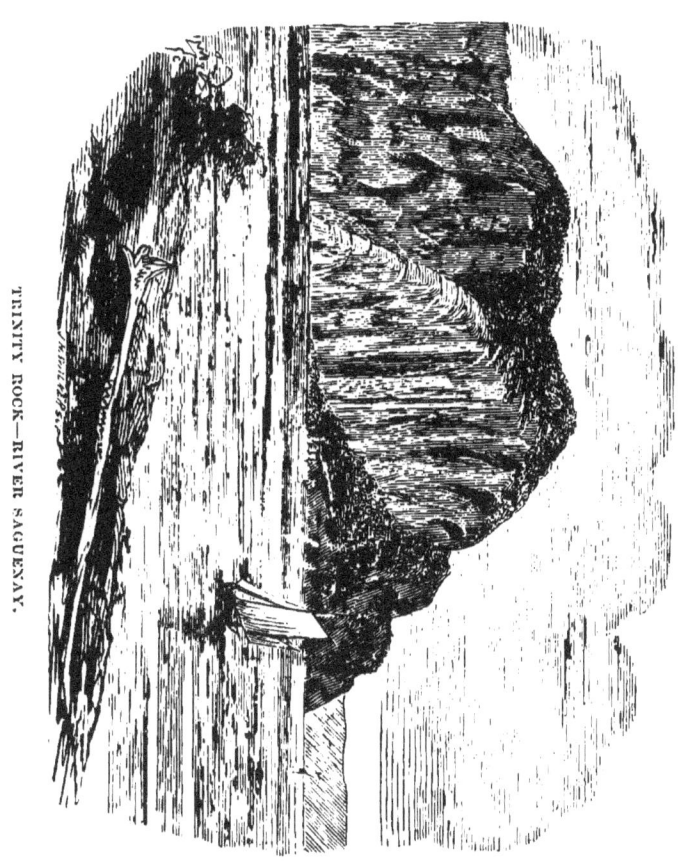

TRINITY ROCK—RIVER SAGUENAY.

foothold and perished with his prey. We also learn from "LeMoine's Oiseaux du Canada," that two or three years ago two fine specimens of the bird of Washington, that rare eagle, were shot here; and indeed continually the flight of the bald-headed eagles along the summits of these beetling cliffs—the salmon leaping after its insect prey—or the seals bobbing their heads out of the water, attract the sportsman's eye.

Nothing can surpass the magnificent salmon fishing of the Marguerite, and other streams, tributaries to the Saguenay, and full particulars with regard to these matters can be obtained at the hotels before leaving Quebec.

CAPE ETERNITY—RIVER SAGUENAY.

Before taking our departure from what must certainly be classed as one of the most lovely and picturesque spots in North America, we would pause to ask the tourist whether his expectations have not been fully realized in every respect, and even far exceeded. We feel satisfied an affirmative answer is the only one that can be given to such a question, for there can be no two opinions as to the magnificence of the scenery brought before the vision on a trip up the River Saguenay to Ha! Ha! Bay. Long descriptions of such scenery can convey but little to the reader and must be at the best very inadequate. The trip must be taken before the grandeur of the Saguenay is to any extent understood and appreciated.

Leaving Tadousac then, on the return journey, the steamer again makes its way across the St. Lawrence to Rivière du Loup, for the convenience of Cacouna passengers, and those desirous, by so arranging it, can here go ashore, and take the train by the Grand Trunk Railway to Quebec. Having sailed down the river, this will prove an interesting change, and bring them into Quebec much earlier. Those remaining on the boat will, if a fine day, enjoy the sail, calling at Murray Bay (Malbaie), as on the downward trip, and afterwards making straight for Quebec. Those tourists taking the train at Rivière du Loup can make connection at Point Levi, which is opposite Quebec, with trains for the White Mountains, the next place at which we purpose stopping with them. Those who still keep to the boat, on arrival at Quebec, will probably prefer lying over a day for rest before proceeding on their journey.

From Point Levi there is not much to be seen, and we therefore advise our traveller as soon as possible to get a sleeping berth in the train, have a good night's rest, and be in good trim on reaching the White Mountains. At Richmond Station, which is the junction with the main line of the Grand Trunk Railway, our tourist can have a comfortable meal at the Station and then change cars, getting on board the train *from* Montreal, which also has a sleeping car attached to it, the train he has travelled by from Quebec being the mail train *for* Montreal.

THE WHITE MOUNTAINS.

A few hours after this he will find himself, after a very pretty ride through a mountainous country, at Gorham, and, on landing, will be almost within arm's length of the door of the " Alpine House," a very good hotel, where he will do well to get himself

WHITE MOUNTAIN RANGE.

ensconced as quickly as possible. From this house, places of interest all about the mountains are within easy distance, and carriages and saddle-horses in great numbers are kept on hand for visiting the various beautiful spots in and around Gorham. There are numerous drives, which are all exceedingly pretty, and indeed the White Mountains are destined to become one of the most fashionable resorts on this continent.

" The White Mountains, or the Switzerland of America, are
" situated in Coos County, New Hampshire, and consist of a
" number of mountain peaks, from four to six thousand feet in
" altitude, the highest of them being Mount Washington, which is
" six thousand two hundred and forty-three feet above the level of
" the sea, and possesses the greatest attraction to tourists. Its
" ascent has lately become quite fashionable with visitors to the
" mountains. It is perhaps impossible to find anything grander
" in mountain scenery than the White Mountains of New Hamp-
" shire. From the 'Alpine House' visitors can proceed by car-
" riages eight miles to the 'Glen House,' which is at the base of
" Mount Washington, and there take saddle-horses for the ascent.
" The 'Notch' is a narrow gorge between two enormous cliffs,
" and extends for a distance of two miles. Its entrance is nearly
" twenty feet wide, and the mountain scenery, diversified by beau-
" tiful cascades falling over perpendicular rocks, is grand in the
" extreme. The 'Willey House' stands in this notch, at an
" elevation of two thousand feet. It is pointed out to the traveller
" as the residence of the Willey family, who perished by an ava-
" lanche from the mountain thirty years ago. In Franconia Notch
" may be seen the Basin and Flume, objects of great interest.
" The Flume is a stream of water having a fall of two hundred
" and fifty feet over fearful precipices into a natural cavity in the
" rocks which forms the basin. The 'Old Man of the Mountain,'
" or profile mountain, is a singularly interesting natural object. It
" obtains its name from the striking resemblance it bears to the
" profile of the human countenance, every feature being marked
" with the greatest accuracy."

Two groups of Mountains are included under the general title

112   ALL ROUND ROUTE AND PANORAMIC GUIDE.

of "The White Hills:" one, the Mount Washington chain or the White Mountains proper,—the other, the Franconia Range, of which Mount Lafayette, a thousand feet lower than Mount Washington, is the highest summit.

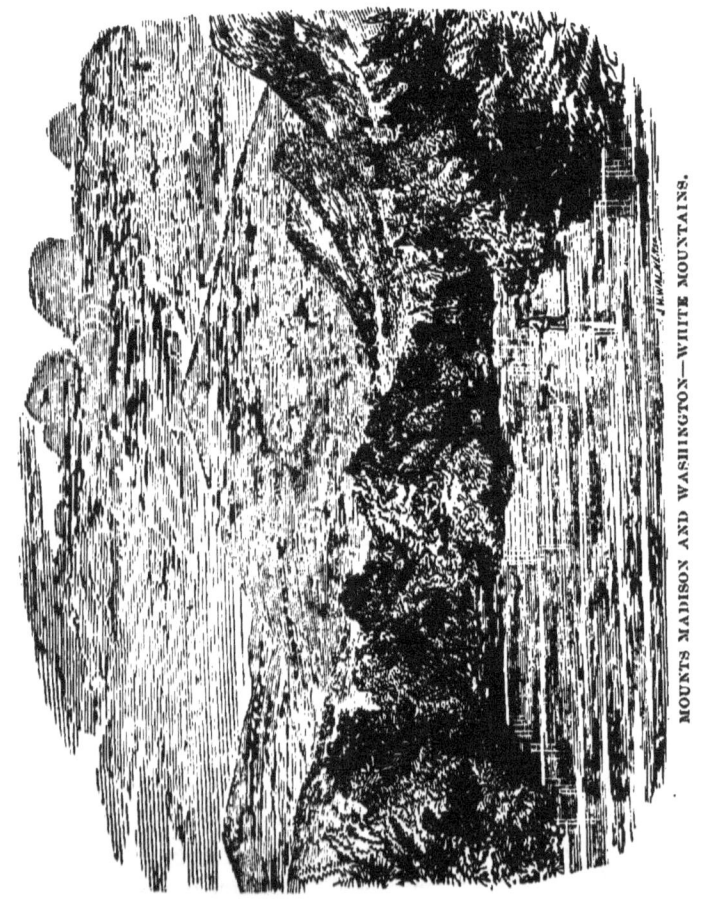

MOUNTS MADISON AND WASHINGTON—WHITE MOUNTAINS.

We extract the following from "The White Hills," (by T. Starr King), a really excellent book:

"There are three paths for the ascent of Mount Washington,— one from the Crawford House at the Notch, one from the White

Mountain House, five miles beyond the Notch, and one from the Glen. The path from the White Mountain House requires the shortest horseback ride. Parties are carried by wagons up the side of Mount Washington to a point less than three miles from the summit. The bridle-path, however, is quite steep, and no time is gained by this ascent. The rival routes are those from the Notch and the Glen. Each of these has some decided advantages over the other. The Glen route is the shortest. For the first four miles the horses keep the wide and hard track, with a regular ascent of one foot in eight, which was laid out for a carriage road to the summit, but never completed. This is a great gain over the corduroy and mud through the forests of Mount Clinton, which belong to the ascent from the Notch.

When we rise up into the region where the real mountain scenery opens, the views from the two paths are entirely different in character, and it is difficult to decide which is grander. From the Notch, as soon as we ride out of the forest, we are on a mountain top. We have scaled Mount Clinton, which is 4,200 feet high. Then the path follows the line of the White Mountain ridge. We descend a little, and soon mount the beautiful dome of Mount Pleasant, which is five hundred feet higher. Descending this to the narrow line of the ridge again, we come to Mount Franklin, a little more than a hundred feet higher than Pleasant, less marked in the landscape, but very difficult to climb. Beyond this, five hundred feet higher still, are the double peaks of Mount Monroe; and then winding down to the Lake of the Clouds, from whence the Ammonoosuc issues, we stand before the cone of Mount Washington, which springs more than a thousand feet above us. The views of the ravines all along this route, as we pass over the sharpest portions of the ridge, and see them sweeping off each way from the path, are very exciting. And there is the great advantage in this approach to be noted, that if Mount Washington is clouded, and the other summits are clear, travellers do not lose the sensations and the effects produced by standing for the first time on a mountain peak.

114   ALL ROUND ROUTE AND PANORAMIC GUIDE.

By the Glen route we cross no subordinate peaks, and do not follow a ridge line from which we see summits towering here and there, but steadily ascend Mount Washington itself. In this way

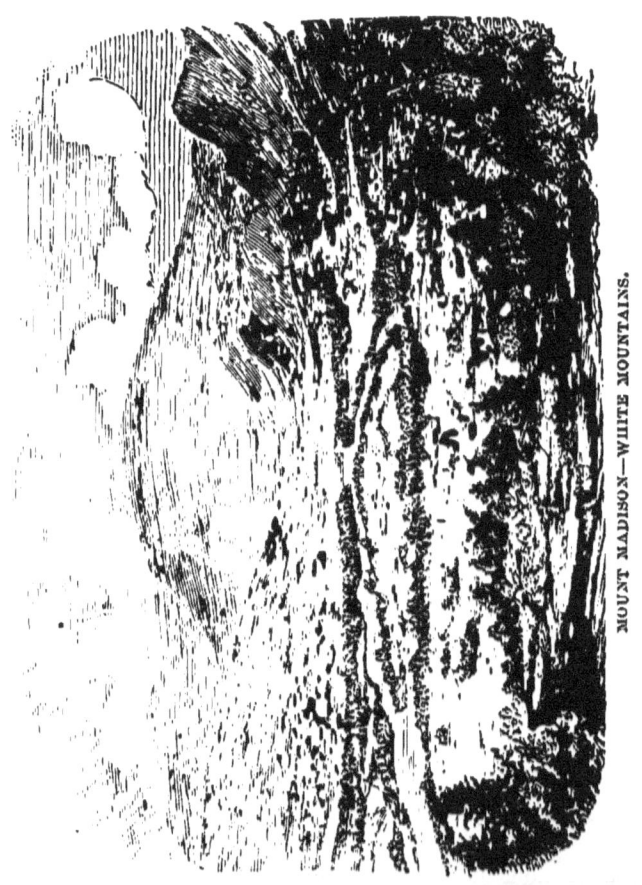

MOUNT MADISON—WHITE MOUNTAINS.

a more adequate conception is gained of its immense mass and majestic architecture. After we pass above the line of the carriage road to the barren portion of the mountain, there are grand pictures at the south and east of the Androscoggin Valley, and the long, heavily wooded Carter range. Indeed, nothing which the day can show will give more astonishment than the spectacle which opens after passing through the spectral forest, made up of acres of trees, leafless, peeled, and bleached, and riding out upon the ledge. Those who make thus their first acquaintance with a

CRAWFORD NOTCH—WHITE MOUNTAINS.

mountain height will feel, in looking down into the immense hollow in which the Glen House is a dot, and off upon the vast green breastwork of Mount Carter, that language must be stretched and intensified to answer for the new sensations awakened. Splendid! glorious! amazing! sublime! with liberal supplies of interjections, are the words that usually gush to the lips; but seldom is an adjective or exclamation uttered that interprets the scene, or coins the excitement and surge of feeling."

Travellers should arrange their plans so as to spend a portion of their time at any rate on the mountains, which they can accomplish by taking up their quarters at the " Glen House." This fine hotel, well known to tourists, has all the comforts of the first class city houses, and being beautifully and conveniently situated, is a most desirable residence for all who intend " doing " the mountains.

Leaving the White Mountains with all their varied attractions we take our seat in the train at Gorham Station for Portland, and find ourselves whizzing along through a magnificent mountainous country, which probably excels anything of its kind in America, and we would recommend a good look out being kept during the journey, for the scenery cannot fail to please. On arrival at South Paris, those desirous have time to obtain refreshments, and those who are accustomed to travel know that it is just as well to take good care of the inner-man, so as to be securely fortified against the fatigue that always, more or less, attends long journeys.

PORTLAND.

After leaving South Paris, nothing of note is seen until a short distance off Portland, when we come in sight of the Atlantic, and feel that sense of pleasure which is experienced on getting near home after a long absence. Arrived at Portland, the principal city of Maine, our tourist will feel that, if not virtually at home, he is at least in its neighborhood, and among friends. To those who have never been in Portland, and can spare the necessary time, we would say, spend a day or two there by all means. It is one of the most pleasant and agreeable cities in the Eastern States, with wide streets and avenues nicely kept, well meriting its title, " The Forest City." Cape Elizabeth is a very favorite resort, and being but a few miles out of the city, an afternoon cannot be better passed than by taking a drive out there. Excursions can also be made to the "Ocean House" and "Orchard Beach," both of which are exceedingly pleasant. Then there are the 365 Islands, including "Cushings," most of which can be reached by ferry-boat or yacht, and where there are always to be found a great many visitors seeking health and relaxation from business. At several of these Islands first-class hotels are to be found, and every comfort can be obtained.

In Portland, "the Falmouth Hotel," kept by Messrs. Ramsay and Wheeler," is an exceedingly fine house and very handsomely furnished. The "Preble House" and "United States Hotel" are both very well kept, equipped with every comfort, and are very desirable houses in every respect. The "St. Julien," which is kept on the "European plan," will also be found a very nice house, well kept, and furnished with every accommodation and convenience for the comfort of its guests.

From Portland, two or three different routes can be chosen, according to the time and inclination of the traveller. If desiring to get to New York direct, and preferring a sea passage, steamers ply regularly, and in fine weather this will be found an exceedingly pleasant trip. We shall, however, presume that the majority travelling intend to go *viâ* Boston, and, if possible, rest a while in that fine city, rather than hurry on at railroad speed, which cannot but prove tiresome. Therefore, to such there is the choice of land or water carriage. Steamers, elegantly furnished, of thorough sea-going qualities, leave Portland every evening for Boston, the passage occupying about ten hours, and, if adopting this mode of conveyance, passengers are landed after a complete night's rest, free from the weariness attending a journey by railway. Those preferring the road, can take the train in the morning, afternoon or evening, there being three trains daily, occupying five hours on the journey.

BOSTON.

Arriving in Boston, we have again got back into the midst of business and excitement, and we see more life than we have witnessed since we sallied forth in our wanderings from New York. Our traveller will doubtless desire to get comfortably quartered during his sojourn here, if only for a brief period, and to do this he has only need to make his way to any of the first-class hotels, given in our advertising columns, where every comfort and luxury is to be met with. There are many things to be visited in and around Boston, but as doubtless our readers will be well acquainted with the city and its surroundings, it is needless to recount all the various places of interest which have been so frequently and lucidly described; albeit we cannot pass hence without advising all those who have never visited Mount Auburn, to do so ere they return home. The Cemetery is indeed a lovely spot, and a few hours is delightfully spent in walking or driving through its beautiful grounds. Here is seen the handiwork too of many a fond heart towards their departed loved ones, and the taste displayed generally has tended to make the place very charming. Harvard University, which is situated at Cambridge, about four miles from Boston, should also be visited. It is here that Longfellow lives, among other American celebrities who have settled down within the shade of their former " Alma Mater." The large organ, in the Boston Music Hall, is visited by great numbers, and performances are given twice a week. If the tourist should be fortunate enough to be in Boston on either day this takes place, he will do well to make a point of attending and enjoying what is a rare treat to all lovers of good music. Information can be obtained at the hotels as to the days and time, and tickets for admission can also be procured.

Leaving Boston, we will now make our way homewards to New York, and deposit the tourist at the place from which we started with him, and in doing this we will again leave him to his choice of routes, as there are several, but, if our opinion be of any use, we would strongly advise him to take the train to Newport, and thence go by one of the magnificent steamers running from that place. This is a lovely trip, and the boats are comfortable in all their appointments, and in ten to twelve hours he will be landed safely in the great city—

NEW YORK.

Here we are again at New York. But before losing ourselves among its 1,200,000 inhabitants we raise our hat to the departing reader with the hope that the trip here ended has been a pleasant one. "On different senses, different objects strike;" but we think there has been something of a sort to please all. Men of every pursuit, and of every variety of taste, will have been able to indulge, each in his peculiar hobby; for although the extent of ground traversed may not seem so large as otherwise might appear, from the similarity of race everywhere encountered, yet, from the free expression given to thought, and the amount of enterprise, social and individual, everywhere met with, there is perhaps not a better field open for examining the working merits of the different schemes which have been from time to time proposed, as affording solutions of the important questions of national education, workmen's associations, co-operative labor, &c., &c.

To the political economist there has been, therefore, abundant subject for fruitful study; and the prospects of an ever-increasing wealth, lately opened by the discovery of rich mineral veins in territory hitherto regarded as unproductive, will afford the theorist grounds on which to work, in conducting his speculations on the great future reserved for this continent.

To the geologist, no tract of country could well be found more replete with interest than that we have traversed. He has been brought face to face with nature in her sublimest aspects; he has been admitted, as it were, to view the *arcana* of her great workshop, and the vast cutting scooped out by the degrading force exerted through successive ages on a limestone formation by a stupendous power like Niagara, to the tiny "striæ" or ice grooves, that to this day mark with unerring line the course of the Northern glaciers, as in ages still more remote they ground down over the greater portion of the North American area.

The artist and sportsman have also no reason to complain of the bill of fare offered for their especial enjoyment. The former could hardly study in a better school than that he has just left—a school that has produced more than one conscientious interpreter of its own peculiar "*genre*;" and of late years none more entitled to our hearty approval than M. Jacobi. And the latter will on his journey round have been able to inspect, in the larger cities, the spoils of many a game bag and fishing basket.

The student of life and character will have occasion to notice many novelties; and the strange mixture of the two languages in Canada, by the "*habitants*," as they are called, will astonish his ideas of euphony. His pure French, if such, perchance, he can command, will not unfrequently prove "*caviare*" to these swarthy folks; but, perhaps, nothing will have more effect on him than the first sight obtained of the red-man, such as he appears in the streets of our cities in this the 19th century. "*O quantum mutatus ab illo*" he will exclaim—from that romantic-looking creature clothed in a scanty allowance of "fig-leaf," who used to be served up for the delectation of our infantile minds in the pages of Old Peter Parley—when he sees the Indian Chief of his boyhood, so strangely modified by the Darwinian system of Natural Selection, into a smooth-faced, oily-haired individual clad in paper collar, Eureka shirt, and extensive wide-awake.

The pages of this our first edition of the new guide will doubtless contain many faults; and alterations in the times of starting and arrival of trains and boats, will naturally continue to be made, irrespective of us; without therefore holding ourselves responsible for any such errors, we will promise to endeavor, in future editions, to make such alterations and corrections as are found necessary from time to time. Any information granted by those best able to afford it—the public—on the *experto crede* principle, will be most readily made use of and acknowledged; and now once more let us greet all our friends with a hearty

FAREWELL

FROM MONTREAL TO NEW YORK DIRECT.

In order to meet all classes of tourists, we have considered it advisable to say a few words in regard to the routes to New York out of Montreal. There are many who may doubtless desire, after making a short stay in Montreal, to return home direct, from lack of time or other causes, to visit the lower St. Lawrence, and, although our Guide proper accompanies the through travellers, a few hints and recommendations to those giving up the tour at Montreal may not come amiss.

Two routes lie at the choice of passengers, one an "all rail," and the other rail and water combined. During the summer season the train by the all rail route, *via* the Vermont Central Railroad, leaves the depot at Montreal at 4.30, p. m., reaching New York about noon the following day. Passengers may travel *via* Troy or Springfield, according as they may elect to take their passages.

The other route referred to is *via* Plattsburgh and Lake Champlain. This is a very favorite way of going to New York, and is so well known and appreciated that little requires to be said in recommendation of it. During the pleasure season trains leave the depot, Montreal, at 5.30, a. m., and 4.40, p. m., for Plattsburg, connecting at that place with the very fine boats of the Champlain Transportation Company for Burlington and Whitehall, at either of which places passengers can again take the train. Those leaving Montreal by the evening train will find it a very pleasant break in the journey to remain over night at Fouquet's Hotel, Plattsburgh, and take the boat the following day. It is a pretty place, and numbers can testify to the fact that a short time occupied at Plattsburgh is well and satisfactorily spent. It is also the "rendezvous" for pleasure parties visiting the "Adirondacks," "Lake George," &c., which are lovely spots and should be seen by all who are lovers of scenery both wild and beautiful. We shall not, however, dwell upon these points of interest, as there are very full and comprehensive guides specially written in regard to these localities, and which are to be readily obtained.

For complete information as to the starting of trains and boats, we would advise tourists to take care and secure a copy of the International Railway and Steam Navigation Guide, which can be had from all news agents, and as the departures may be altered during the season, it is impossible we can hold ourselves responsible for the continued correctness of the times given by us. They will, however, be as accurate as is possible with such details.

DETROIT AND CHICAGO.

As in all likelihood many of our tourists, who have never visited the large Western cities, may desire, whilst at Niagara, to take a run—even if only for a brief period—to the principal business localities in the Western States, we have thought it desirable, and as a matter of convenience to the travelling public, to refer in a very few words to one or two places in the Western States of America, which are not only worthy, and will amply compensate for any time spent in visiting them, but which really ought to be seen, and well seen, by all those who consider themselves travellers. It is needless to say that we refer to the fine cities of DETROIT, in the State of Michigan, and CHICAGO, in the State of Illinois. A few hours' ride from Suspension Bridge through a pleasant country, over the Great Western Railway, will bring the tourist to the town of Windsor, in Canada, and a few minutes more occupied in crossing the river by the Steam Ferry, will land him in the fine city of Detroit. This city, like most of those in the West, has its principal streets running at right angles, and strangers are at no loss to find their way about. It contains some exceedingly fine buildings, parks and streets. As regards hotel accommodation, we can confidently recommend either the "Biddle" House, on Jefferson Avenue, or the "Russell" House on

Woodward Avenue, as first-class hotels, containing all the modern improvements, with every comfort required by the most fastidious. We would advise a visit to the pretty cemetery, and the outskirts of the city, which in all directions are very fine, and will well repay a drive, or a long " constitutional."

The next and other place which we wish the Tourist to visit, is the "New York" of the West, CHICAGO. Probably most of our pleasure seekers may have already visited the lion city of the West; but to those who have not made the journey within the last few years, we would say, by all means extend your absence from home, and postpone your journey eastward, for at least a few days, and go and see the march of progress being made by our Western friends. Take the Michigan Southern, or the Michigan Central Railway at Detroit, and after ten hours of as comfortable travelling as can be obtained on the Continent, you will find yourself in Chicago. Either of the routes named out of Detroit may be selected by the tourist with every confidence, as the time occupied on the journey is about equal, and the scenery along the routes very pleasing.

The Michigan Southern and Northern Indiana Railroad runs from Chicago to Toledo and Detroit,—was completed from Monroe to Hillsdale, 106 miles, in December, 1846, and cars ran through to Chicago, in May, 1852. The total length of the road, and all its branches, is 535 miles. The Depot in Chicago is corner of Van Buren and Sherman streets.

The Michigan Central Road was opened to Kalamazoo, 143 miles from Detroit, February 1st, 1846. The road was open to Michigan City, October 30, 1850, and to Chicago, May 21, 1852. The total length of the road is 284 miles. The depot in Chicago is at the foot of Lake-street.

It is truly wonderful, the strides that have been made in Chicago of late years. It is not necessary to recount the particulars of how Chicago has grown in numbers and wealth within a very limited period; all who have even heard of the place are also acquainted in a greater or less degree with the marvellous manner in which the city has risen to its present status, as the Commercial emporium of the West. Chicago, however, must be seen, to be appreciated properly, and one cannot visit the City without feeling that a current of vitality courses through the veins of all its people. As regards hotels, both the "Tremont" and "Sherman" are fine houses, and our tourist will find every accommodation and comfort at either. There are a number of very fine buildings in the city, and many pleasant drives, but as these are fully enumerated and described in the Guides to the City, published in Chicago, we shall not particularise them.

In returning to the East, if our tourist will spare the time, a most enjoyable and healthful trip may be made by taking the rail to Milwaukee, and there crossing Lake Michigan by one of the Detroit and Milwaukee Company's very fine steamers to Grand Haven, where they connect with the railway owned by that Company, running to Detroit. From our own experience we can truly say, that in fine weather this is a most lovely journey, besides varying the route. From Detroit the Great Western Railway will convey the tourist back to Suspension Bridge (Niagara Falls.)

CANADA.

GEOGRAPHICAL, POLITICAL, AND STATISTICAL, &c

The Province of Canada, in 1791, or as it was then termed, The Province of Quebec, by the terms of the Act of 31 Geo. III, chap. 31, was divided into the two Governments of Upper and Lower Canada, with representative institutions for each; the Lower Province was under a Governor, whilst the Upper was under a Lieutenant-Governor. This Constitution was suspended in consequence of the rebellion in Upper Canada in 1838, and a Special Council appointed. In 1840 the two Provinces were re-united—by an Act 3rd and 4th Victoria, chapter 36—and the

Legislative Councils of the United Provinces were consolidated. Nova Scotia and New Brunswick were united with Canada under the title of the Dominion of Canada, by an Act of Parliament passed on March 29, 1867.

The population of United Canada in the year 1800 was estimated at 240,000; in 1825 it amounted to 581,920; and in 1857 to 1,842,265. The population of the Dominion of Canada, according to the census taken in the year 1861, was 3,090,561..

Upper Canada	1,396,091
Lower Canada	1,111,566
Nova Scotia	330,857
New Brunswick	252,047
Total	3,090,561.

The estimated population is now over 4,000,000.

The number of members of each of the great branches of Religious Denominations, Roman Catholic and Protestant, (including the Anglican Church and Dissenters,) according to the census of 1861, was as follows:—

Upper Canada—Roman Catholics, 258,141; Protestants, 1,135,950. Lower Canada—Roman Catholics, 943,253; Protestants, 268,313. Giving a total of Roman Catholics, 1,201,394; Protestants, 1,404,263.

The population of the principal cities in the Dominion of Canada was, by the census of 1861—

Upper Canada, now the Province of Ontario,	Toronto	44,821
	Hamilton	19,096
	Kingston	13,743
	Ottawa	14,696
	London	11,555
Lower Canada, now the Province of Quebec,	Montreal	90,323
	Quebec	51,109
Nova Scotia	Halifax	25,026
New Brunswick	St. John	27,317

Of course the population of many of these places has largely increased since the census was taken; Montreal, for instance, has now about 130,000 inhabitants.

According to the estimates of the year 1867, British North America (extending from the Pacific to the Atlantic) had a population of nearly 4,250,000, giving, on a territory of 619,362 English square miles, not quite seven individuals to the square mile.

It may be interesting to tourists to state the mean temperature during the months of travel, when the navigation is open from the lakes to the ocean. In June it is 64° Fahrenheit. In July it is 68°. In August it is 65°. In September 58°. The mean of the above four months being 64°, and the mean of the whole year being 42°.

THE END.

TOURIST TICKETS. **GRAND TRUNK RAILWAY.** SEASON 1870.

RATES OF FARE FROM NIAGARA FALLS.

No. of Form	DESTINATION.	ROUTE.	Through Fare from Niagara Falls.
			$ cts.
9	Alpine House, GORHAM	Via Montreal, Quebec and G. T. R.	22.00
13	Do.	Via Montreal and G. T. R. direct	19.00
11	BOSTON	" Montreal, Quebec, Gorham and Portland.	25.00
12	Do.	" Montreal, St. Johns, Vermont Central and Rutland & Burlington R.R.	22.00
15	Do.	" Montreal, Gorham and Portland	22.00
16	Do.	" Montreal, St. Johns and Vermont Central Line	22.00
17	Do.	" Ogdensburg, St. Albans and Vermont Central Line	18.00
29	Do.	" Montreal, Plattsburg, Lake Champlain to Whitehall, Saratoga, Rutland, Bellows' Falls and Fitchburg	26.00
34	Do.	" Montreal, Plattsburg, Lake Champlain, Lake George, Saratoga, People's Line of Steamers to New York, and Sound Steamers to Boston	32.00
35	Do.	" Montreal, St. Johns, White River Junction, Wells River, Littleton, Stages to and from Profile House and Crawford House, and Rail via Concord, Nashua, and Lowell to Boston	38.50
38	Do.	" Montreal, Plattsburg, Lake Champlain, Burlington, Bellows' Falls & Fitchburg	22.00
39	Do.	" Ogdensburg, Plattsburg, Lake Champlain, Burlington, Bellows' Falls and Fitchburg	18.00
40	CRAWFORD HOUSE	" Montreal, St. Johns, White River Junction, Wells River and Littleton	28.00
50	Do.	" Ogdensburg, St. Albans, White River Junction, Wells River and Littleton	22.50
2	KINGSTON	" Rail or Steamer	8.00
6	MONTREAL	" Rail or Steamer	13.00
19	NEW YORK	" Montreal, Plattsburg, Lake Champlain, Lake George, Saratoga and Hudson River R.R.	28.50
20	Do.	" Montreal, Plattsburg, Lake Champlain, Lake George, Saratoga & People's Line Steamers	27.40
21	Do.	" Montreal, Plattsburg, Lake Champlain, Whitehall, Saratoga and Hudson River R.R.	25.60
22	Do.	" Montreal, Plattsburg, Lake Champlain, Whitehall, Saratoga and People's Line Steamers	24.50
24	Do.	" Montreal, Gorham, Portland and Boston.	37.00
25	Do.	" Montreal, Quebec, Gorham, Portland and Boston	30.00
26	Do.	" Montreal, Plattsburg, Lake Champlain, Lake George, Saratoga and Day Line Steamers	27.40
27	Do.	" Montreal, Plattsburg, Lake Champlain, Whitehall, Saratoga and Day Line Steamers	24.50
36	Do.	" Montreal, Quebec, Gorham, over the White Mountains to Littleton, then via Concord, Nashua and Boston	48.00
37	Do.	" Montreal, Quebec, Sherbrooke, Lake Magog to Newport, Littleton, Stages to and from Profile House and Crawford House, then via Concord, Nashua and Boston	48.0
42	Do.	" Montreal, St. Johns, Burlington, Lake Champlain, Whitehall, Saratoga and Day Line Steamers	21.5

Rates of Fare from Niagara Falls.—*Continued.*

No. of Form	DESTINATION.	ROUTE.	Through Fare from Niagara Falls.
43	NEW YORK	"Montreal, St. Johns, Burlington, Lake Champlain, Lake George, Saratoga, and Day Line Steamers	27.40
44	Do.	"Ogdensburg, St. Albans, Burlington. Lake Champlain, Whitehall, Saratoga and Day Line Steamers	20.50
45	Do.	"Ogdensburg, St. Albans, Burlington, Lake Champlain, Lake George, Saratoga and Day Line Steamers	23.40
46	Do.	"Montreal, St. Johns, Burlington, Bellows' Falls and Springfield	23.00
51	Do.	"Ogdensburg, St. Albans, White River Junction and Springfield	19.00
5	OGDENSBURG	"Rail or Steamer	10.00
4	PRESCOTT	"Rail or Steamer	10.00
10	PORTLAND	"Montreal, Quebec and Gorham	23.00
14	Do.	"Montreal and Gorham direct	20.00
40	Do. & Back to N. FALLS	"Montreal and Gorham, and return by G. T. R.	29.00
47	PROFILE HOUSE	"Montreal, St. Johns, White River Junction, Wells River, and Stage from Littleton	23.00
48	Do.	"Ogdensburg, St. Albans, White River Junction, Wells River and Stage from Littleton	19.00
7	QUEBEC	"Rail or Steamer	15.50
8	Do. & Back to MONTREAL	"Rail or Steamer	18.00
18	SARATOGA	"Montreal, Plattsburg, Lake Champlain and Lake George	23.50
23	Do.	"Montreal, Plattsburg, Lake Champlain and Whitehall	20.65
28	Do.	"Montreal, Gorham, Stages from Alpine House to Glen House, Crawford House, Profile House and Littleton, then Rail to White River Junction and Burlington, and *via* Lake Champlain and Lake George and Moreau Station to Saratoga.	46.75
52	Do.	"Montreal, St. Johns, Burlington, Lake Champlain and Whitehall	20.65
53	Do.	"Montreal, St. Johns, Burlington, Lake Champlain and Lake George	23.50
54	Do.	"Ogdensburg, St. Albans, Burlington, Lake Champlain and Whitehall	16.65
55	Do.	"Ogdensburg, St. Albans, Burlington, Lake Champlain and Lake George	19.50
41	MONTREAL to QUEBEC and Back	"Rail or Steamer	5.00
56	RICHMOND to QUEBEC and Back	"G. T. R.	3.00

The Coupons between Niagara Falls and Toronto, Toronto and Kingston, Kingston and Prescott, Prescott and Montreal, and Montreal and Quebec, are valid either by Boat or Rail, and they are likewise good by either the South Shore Express Line of Steamers or by the Royal Mail Line, which continues to run from Toronto as heretofore.

The Tickets include Meals and State-Rooms on Lake Ontario and the River St. Lawrence, as far as Montreal, but between Montreal and Quebec they are for Passage only.

No deviation from the above Rates will be allowed without special authority.

HENRY SHACKELL,
General Passenger Agent G.T.R

Montreal, May, 1870.

Biddle House,
JEFFERSON AVENUE,
DETROIT, MICH.

THIS

FIRST-CLASS HOTEL

HAS RECENTLY BEEN

Enlarged, Beautified and Re-Furnished,

AND HAS CAPACITY FOR ACCOMMODATING

FIVE HUNDRED GUESTS.

May 1st. A. B. TABER,
 Proprietor.

Russell House,
DETROIT.

WITBECK & CHITTENDEN,
PROPRIETORS.

THIS

FIRST-CLASS HOTEL

IS SITUATED ON

WOODWARD'S AVENUE,

FRONTING CAMPUS MARTIUS,

OPPOSITE NEW CITY HALL

AND

DETROIT OPERA HOUSE,

Has been refitted and refurnished.

Superb Accommodation for 400 Guests.

Michigan Southern Railroad.

DETROIT TO CHICAGO.

Passengers from Canada and the Eastern States, for
Chicago and all Points in the Great West,
GOING VIA DETROIT,
SHOULD BE SURE TO PURCHASE TICKETS
BY THE
MICHIGAN SOUTHERN RAILROAD
The Shortest, Quickest, and Most Comfortable Route.

Passengers by this Line secure all the modern improvements adopted for their

SECURITY AND COMFORT,
AND HAVE
Quick Time and Sure Connections.

Elegant Sleeping Coaches on all Night Trains.

Palace Coaches & Smoking Cars on Day Trains.

First-Class Eating Houses at Convenient Points, and Ample Time Allowed for Meals.

Through Tickets and Checks for Baggage, via the MICHIGAN SOUTHERN RAILROAD, can be obtained at all the principal Ticket Offices in the United States and Canada.

JAMES BROWN, F. E. MORSE,
Passenger Agent, General Passenger Agent,
DETROIT, MICH. CHICAGO, ILLINOIS.

The Popular Route to the West
BY THE

1870 **Michigan Central R. R.**

FROM
DETROIT TO CHICAGO.

Four Express Passenger Trains run each way daily.

The Day Trains have Cars especially for Ladies, and Luxurious Smoking Cars for Gentlemen.

All the Cars have SIX-WHEELED TRUCKS, and are fitted up with every modern improvement for the safety and comfort of Travellers.

NIGHT TRAINS
HAVE
Pullman's Palace Sleeping and Refreshment Cars,
UNSURPASSED FOR COMFORT AND ELEGANCE.
THE VENTILATION AND BEDDING ARE PERFECT.

☞ **FOR EMIGRANTS** ☜

This line possesses unequalled advantages for
CHEAP, SPEEDY, AND COMFORTABLE TRANSIT.

Spacious Bathing Rooms on the Dock at Detroit,
AND SPECIAL ATTENTION GIVEN TO THIS CLASS
OF TRAVELLERS.

H. E. SARGENT,
General Superintendent,
CHICAGO, ILL.

All-Round Route Map.

EXCURSION ROUTES
VIA
NIAGARA FALLS,

Toronto, Ottawa, Montreal, Quebec,

White Mountains, Portland,

LAKE CHAMPLAIN, LAKE GEORGE, &C.

Everett House,

Union Square, - - - - - - - New York.
ON THE EUROPEAN PLAN.

This MAGNIFICENT HOTEL is eligibly situated, fronting the north side of Union Square, and in the immediate vicinity of the Academy of Music, Wallack's Theatre, Booth's Dramatic Temple, Fifth Avenue Theatre, Academy of Design, Young Men's Christian Association, Grace Church, and other places of attraction, and is particularly recommended to Tourists, Travellers and families who desire the quiet and refinement of an Hotel, select in its character, first-class in all its appointments and easy of access to the best places of amusement as well as to the business portion of the Metropolis.

WM. B. BORROWS, Proprietor.

THE CONTINENTAL HOTEL LONG BRANCH, N. J., will be opened for the season of 1870 on the 15th of June, and has accommodation for nearly One Thousand Guests. This famous watering place is world-renowned for the purity of the air and its superior Sea Bathing, and is the resort of the Fashion, Wealth and Intelligence of the Country. Only one hour and a-half's journey from New York City, and several Steamers Daily.

WM. B. BORROWS, Proprietor.

Illustrated Books for Tourists
IN AMERICA,
PUBLISHED BY
VIRTUE & YORSTON,
10 AND 12 DEY STREET, NEW YORK,
55 AND 57 YONGE STREET, TORONTO

A GUIDE TO THE HUDSON,
FROM THE WILDERNESS TO THE SEA.
BY BENSON J. LOSSING,
Author of "Pictorial History of the Civil War," "Field-Book of the Revolution," "Field-Book of the War of 1812," &c., &c.

Illustrated by upwards of Three Hundred Engravings, on Wood and Steel, from Drawings by the Author.

One volume, small quarto, morocco cloth, gilt............................$10 00
"   "   morocco extra,................................ 15 00

"Very few Americans are so well qualified as is Mr. Lossing to write intelligently regarding the Hudson, and every American will bear testimony to the conscientious accuracy of the illustrations."—*New York Daily Times.*

"Mr. Lossing writes, as he draws, with singular felicity, and his pages have an unflagging interest which rarely attaches to books of mere description."—*Albany Evening Journal.*

UNITED STATES SCENERY.
Land, Lake, and River Scenery in the United States, Illustrated in a Series of 120 Beautiful Steel Engravings, from Sketches made for the purpose, by W H. Bartlett. The descriptions by N. P. Willis.
Two volumes in one, full morocco,...................................... $25 00

CANADIAN SCENERY.
Land, Lake, and River Scenery of the Dominion of Canada, Illustrated in a Series of 118 Fine Steel Engravings, from Sketches by W. H. Bartlett. The descriptions by N. P. Willis.
Two volumes in one, full morocco,...................................... $25 00
Any of the above works sent by Mail or Express prepaid on receipt of the amount.

ALSO,
The following works on European Scenery for Tourists on the Continent:

SCENERY AND ANTIQUITIES OF IRELAND.
Illustrated in 120 Engravings on Steel, from Original Drawings made expressly for this work by W. H. Bartlett. Historical and Descriptive Text by J. Stirling Coyne and N. P. Willis.
Two volumes in one, morocco extra...................................... $25 00
Two volumes, half morocco... 25 00
Two volumes, full morocco... 30 00

SCOTLAND ILLUSTRATED.
A Series of 120 Engravings on Steel, from Drawings by Horatio McCulloch, Thomas Allom, and W. H. Bartlett. Descriptions by W. Beattie, M.D.
Two volumes in one, morocco extra..................................... $25 00
Catalogues of all our Illustrated Works sent on application.

VIRTUE & YORSTON,
10 and 12 Dey Street, New York.

HUDSON RIVER BY DAYLIGHT.
1870.

ALBANY AND NEW YORK
DAY LINE OF STEAMBOATS.

On and after June 1st, one of the splendid and justly celebrated Steamers,

C. Vibbard and Daniel Drew,

Will leave NEW YORK and ALBANY every Morning, Sundays excepted, landing at

YONKERS,
   WEST POINT,
      CORNWALL,
         NEWBURG,
            POUGHKEEPSIE,
               RHINEBECK,
                  CATSKILL,
                     HUDSON,

CONNECTING WITH TRAINS OF

New York Central, Albany and Susquehanna,
AND
RENSSELAER AND SARATOGA RAILROADS.

ISAAC L. WELSH
GENERAL TICKET AGENT,
Albany, N. Y.

THE STANDARD

American Billiard Table,

The Best and only Reliable Tables Manufactured;

ALSO,

ALL ARTICLES PERTAINING TO THE TRADE,

FOR SALE BY

PHELAN & COLLENDER,

NO. 738 BROADWAY, NEW YORK.

Agent for Canada:

CHAS. B. CHADWICK,

At the BILLIARD HALL,   207 ST. JAMES STREET,

MONTREAL,

Where there are sixteen tables, and where all goods of the above manufacture can be obtained.

AMERICAN HOTEL,

Near the Steamboat and Railroad depots,

DAVID WALKER,

PROPRIETOR,

Corner of Yonge and Front Streets,

TORONTO, ONT.

Tourists will find this an exceedingly

COMFORTABLE HOUSE.   **TERMS MODERATE.**

STEAMER

"CITY OF  TORONTO."
Quickest and Most   Pleasant Route between

TORONTO and BUFFALO

VIA NIAGARA FALLS.

The Steamer "CITY OF TORONTO," (Capt. D. MILLOY), during the Summer Season, will make two trips daily between Toronto, Niagara and Lewiston, in connection with the New York Central Railway.

    Leave TORONTO,   7.00 A.M.,   2.30 P.M.
    "   LEWISTON,   11.00 "   6.00 "

Time between Toronto and Buffalo only four and a-half hours.

N. MILLOY, *Agent*,
Toronto, May, 1870.   No. 8 Front Street.

B. SAUNDERS,

MERCHANT TAILOR, ROBE MAKER, &C.,
Romaine Buildings,
KING STREET, WEST,
TORONTO.

F. MORISON,
Merchant and Military Tailor,
12 KING STREET WEST,
TORONTO.

Great Central Route.

GREAT WESTERN RAILWAY OF CANADA.

AND

United States Mail Route, from Toronto, Suspension Bridge, Niagara Falls,

TO

DETROIT, MICHIGAN,

WITH BRANCH LINES FROM

Hamilton to Toronto, from Harrisburgh to Guelph, from Komoka to Sarnia, and from Wyoming to Petrolia,

FORMING WITH ITS CONNECTIONS THE

SHORTEST AND BEST ROUTE BETWEEN ALL POINTS EAST & WEST.

This is the only route via Niagara Falls, and passengers are enabled to view the FALLS OF NIAGARA while crossing the MAMMOTH SUSPENSION BRIDGE in the Cars of this Railway.

FOUR THROUGH EXPRESS TRAINS EACH WAY, DAILY.

The line offers unsurpassed facilities for the conveyance of Emigrants, and affords them superior comforts in Cars, and bathing and washing rooms, &c.

Eastward bound Trains connect regularly at Suspension Bridge with Trains on the New York Central Railway for Buffalo, Rochester, Syracuse, Rome, Ogdensburgh, Utica, Albany, Philadelphia, New York, Boston, Baltimore, Washington, and the principal points in New England and the Eastern States; at Toronto with the Northern Railway for Collingwood, and the Grand Trunk Railway for Montreal, Quebec and Portland.

Westward bound Trains connect at Detroit with Trains on the Michigan Central, Detroit and Milwaukee, and Michigan Southern Railroads, for Chicago, Galena, Dubuque, Milwaukee, Rock Island, St. Louis, St. Paul, Cairo, Burlington, Lacrosse, Saginaw, Cincinnati, Memphis, Vicksburg, New Orleans, Omaha, Denver, Salt Lake, San Francisco, all California points, and all important places in the West, North-West and South-West.

CLOSE connections made at TORONTO with GRAND TRUNK RAILWAY and during Lake Navigation at Hamilton and Toronto with

ROYAL MAIL LINE OF STEAMERS

For all important points on Lake Ontario and the River St. Lawrence.

The only All-rail Route to the Oil Regions of Canada.

Pullman's Patent 16 Wheeled Palace Sleeping Cars,

Which for elegance and comfort are not surpassed, run through between New York and Chicago, Rochester and Chicago and Rochester and Detroit without change, connecting with Palace Car Line on Western roads to St. Louis, Omaha, California, &c.

W. K. MUIR,
General Superintendent, Hamilton, Ontario.

This Splendid Commodious Hotel (opened by the undersigned on the 1st August, 1867,) is finished and furnished with every regard to comfort and luxury; has hot and cold water, with Baths, and Bed-rooms are large and well ventilated, and arranged for private parties and families. The aim has been to make this the most unexceptionable first-class Hotel in Canada.

The undersigned trusts that his long experience in the CLIFTON HOUSE at Niagara Falls will give confidence to his friends and the travelling public that they will receive every attention and comfort, with reasonable charges, at this his new and elegant House.

G. P. SHEARS, Lessee & Manager

Thos MᶜGaw. } MANAGERS
Mark H. Irish. }

Capt. Thomas Dick
Proprietor.

The QUEEN'S HOTEL, in the City of Toronto, is one of the largest in the Dominion of Canada, situated on Front Street, overlooking the beautiful Bay and Lake Ontario, is convenient to Railway Stations, Steamboat Piers, and the business part of the City.

The Rooms are commodious and fitted up with new furniture in most modern style. An elegant Billiard Parlor in the House. The grounds around it being both spacious and airy with Croquet Lawns, &c., renders it one of the most pleasant and desirable Hotels for business men, pleasure seekers and the travelling public.

The Tourists will find much to interest them in the City.

The Queen's Park, The University buildings, The Lunatic Asylum, The Trinity College, and the Normal School, with its extensive Galleries of Art; together with pleasant drives and extensive views of a varied character.

Carriages always in waiting.

Thos M!Gaw. } MANAGERS
Mark H. Irish.

Capt. Thomas Dick,
Proprietor.

(THE QUEEN'S) ROYAL NIAGARA HOTEL is located in the Town of Nigara, in a beautiful grove at the mouth of Niagara River on the shore of Lake Ontario, fourteen miles from Niagara Falls and twelve miles from St. Catharines; is accessible by Railway and Steamboat; only thirty minutes ride by the Erie and Niagara Railway, or the New York Central Railroad via Lewiston, N. Y., from Niagara Falls, and two hours by Steamer from Toronto.

The Building has just been erected, and newly and elegantly furnished throughout; is a branch house of the QUEEN'S HOTEL, Toronto, and to be open for Guests during the summer season.

One of the Royal Mail Line of Steamers leaves Niagara Daily for Montreal, passing through Lake Ontario, the Thousand Islands, the Rapids and River St. Lawrence, calling at all points, both on the Canadian and American shores.

The Town of Niagara was at one time the Seat of Government for Upper Canada; its surroundings are full of varied and historical interests.

The facilities for Black Bass and other Fishing, Bathing and Boating unsurpassed.

The Drives are refreshing, and the Scenery beautiful in and about the Town, and along the banks of the Lake and River.

Special arrangements can be made with families desiring board for the season

REVERE HOUSE

BOWDOIN SQUARE
BOSTON,
WRISLEY, WETHERBEE & Co.   PROPRIETORS

We respectfully invite your attention to the Revere House, which has just been refurnished and modernized by the introduction of water, bathing rooms, &c., at an expense of more than seventy-five thousand dollars.

The Public will find unsurpassed accmomodations in the single and suites of rooms, which afford attractive home comforts.

Mr. Tyler B. Gaskill, one of the Partner, is Caterers, whose reputation in that line is widely known to the patrons of the Revere during the past fifteen years.

The Revere is pleasantly situated near the principal lines of travel, and in close proximity to business.

Mr. Gardner Wetherbee, late of the Fifth Avenue Hotel, New York, has become one of the Proprietors, and will be pleased to welcome the Travelling Public at the Revere House.

        WRISLEY, WETHERBEE & CO., Proprietors.

Boston, May, 1870.

WAVERLEY HOUSE
CHARLESTON SQUARE,
BOSTON, MASS.

Five Minutes walk from the Railroad Depots, and only fifteen minutes walk from the Boston Post Office. Horse Cars pass the House every minute. Cost of Carriage hire from depots to the Hotel refunded at the House. **Board cheaper than any other First-Class Hotel in Boston.**

THIS SPLENDID HOTEL is one of the largest in New England, containing nearly 500 rooms, which overlook the harbor and surrounding towns. Its elegant dining room will seat 250 at its tables. The House will accommodate nearly 1000 people. The rooms are large, and furnished with velvet and Brussels carpeting and elegant black walnut furniture. Soft water is carried to every sleeping room, and each has also a closet six feet square, making it very convenient for family boarding. Bathing rooms and water closets on every floor. The whole House is kept at a moderate temperature in winter by steam, the boilers for which are in a building outside of the House. In summer the House is cool, as there is nothing to obstruct the free circulation of air. The WAVERLEY HOUSE has elegant parlors, consisting of several rooms, extending 220 feet, all fronting on a public square of two acres, in the centre of which is a fountain, surrounded by a lawn. The tables are supplied with the best materials that the market affords, and first-class Cooks serve them in the best style. There are also an elegant billiard hall and an elegant barber's shop in the House. Those who once visit the WAVERLEY HOUSE, will ever after make it their home when they visit Boston, as it is the most convenient to reach, and the most home-like of any hotel in the City. Those who arrive in Boston by the cars can take a coach and order it to drive to the WAVERLEY HOUSE, and the cost of so doing will be refunded at the House.

Letters in regard to the House can be addressed to
WAVERLEY HOUSE, Charleston Square, Boston, Mass.

"AMERICAN,"
BOSTON.

LEWIS RICE & SON.

The Largest First-Class Hotel
IN THE CITY.

Tuft's Improved Passenger elevator. | Family suites and single apartments, with Bathing and water conveniences adjoining. | Billiard Halls, Telegraph Office and Café.

PARKER HOUSE,
School Street,
BOSTON.

HARVEY D. PARKER.   JOHN F. MILLS.

350 NOTRE DAME STREET, MONTREAL.

ROYAL PATRONAGE.

TAILOR TO

H. R. H. PRINCE ARTHUR.

J. WHITTAKER,
LATE MASTER TAILOR TO THE 4th BATTALION RIFLE BRIGADE,
350 NOTRE DAME STREET,
☞ ONLY FIRST-CLASS TAILORING. LADIES' RIDING HABITS AND JACKETS.

THE ST. LAWRENCE AND OTTAWA RAILWAY

FROM PRESCOTT,

On the River St. Lawrence, Opposite Ogdensburgh

TO

OTTAWA CITY,

THE CAPITAL OF THE DOMINION OF CANADA.

On arrival at Prescott or Ogdensburgh the Tourist can leave the Steamer or the Railway, and proceed thence by the St. Lawrence and Ottawa Railway, a distance of 54 miles, to the City of OTTAWA, the Seat of the Government of Canada.
The magnificent Parliamentary Buildings, the Falls of the Chaudière, the extensive Lumbering and other Mills there, the celebrated Timber Slides, and the Military Canal Works, surrounded by scenery of unusual grandeur, form a combination of attractions, rarely met with by the Tourist.

GOING NORTH.

PRESCOTT TO OTTAWA.

DISTANCE.	STATIONS.	No. 1 MAIL.	No. 3 MAIL.
		P. M.	A. M.
	Prescott.................................	1.30	7.10
2	Prescott Junction.........................	1.45	7.30
9	*Spencerville	2.00	7.55
16¼	*Oxford...................................	2.20	8.30
22½	Kemptville	2.40	8.50
31	*Osgoode.................................	3.00	9.20
37	Rossiters.................................	3.15	9.40
43	*Gloucester..............................	3.30	10.00
54	Ottawa...................................	4.00	10.30

GOING SOUTH.

OTTAWA TO PRESCOTT.

DISTANCE.	STATIONS.	No. 2 MAIL.	No. 4 MAIL.
		A. M.	P. M.
	Ottawa...................................	7.00	12.15
11	*Gloucester..............................	7.25	12.55
17	Rossiters.................................	7.40	1.15
23	*Osgoode.................................	7.55	1 35
31½	Kemptville	8.15	2.05
37¼	*Oxford...................................	8.30	2.20
45	*Spencerville	8.50	2.45
52	Prescott Junction.........................	9.10	3.15
54	Prescott.................................	9.25	3 20

NOTE.—Trains are run by Montreal Time.

The Russell House,
OTTAWA.

THIS ESTABLISHMENT IS SITUATED ON THE

CORNER OF SPARKS AND ELGIN STREETS,

In the very centre of the City, and the immediate neighborhood of the

Parliament and Departmental Buildings, the Post Office, the Custom House, the City Hall, the Theatre, the Telegraph Office, and the different Banks.

THE PARLIAMENTARY BUILDINGS,

From their position and architectural design, should be visited by

THE TOURIST.

The scenery and natural curiosities of the Upper Ottawa, the beautiful FALLS OF THE CHAUDIERE and of the RIDEAU RIVER, the Timber Slides, the extensive Water-power, and the Lumbering and other Mills, are within easy reach of the City, and form a combination of attraction unsurpassed in Canada.

The Russell House is fitted up and conducted with every regard to comfort, and will accommodate no fewer than 250 guests, constituting it one of the largest Hotels in Canada.

JAMES A. GOUIN,
Proprietor.

KINGSTON, ONT.

Captain H. E. SWALES, Proprietor.

This well Established and Popular Hotel has been recently re-fitted and re-furnished by the present Proprietor, and for spaciousness of accommodation and elegance of arrangements holds a first position in the Dominion.

Situated as Kingston is, at the foot of Lake Ontario and the beautiful bay of Quinte, and at the head of River St. Lawrence, closely adjacent to the American Border, in the vicinity of which are the "Penitentiary" and the "Rockwood Lunatic Asylum," having military fortifications, second only to those of Quebec, it presents attractions which necessarily invite Tourists and pleasure seekers, and, consequently, render it highly essential to have our Hotel at once easy of access and popularly recommended.

Passengers, by taking the Grand Trunk Rail from Toronto, in the morning, arrive here at 1 p.m., will have an opportunity of visiting the places of interest in and around the City, can then, after a good night's rest, take the Steamer at 5.30 a.m., passing through the "Thousand Islands" and "Rapids" of the River St. Lawrence, arriving in Montreal the same morning.

The wharf of the Canadian Express and Mail Line Steamers is within two minutes walk of the Hotel. Passengers and baggage are taken down to the Steamers free of charge.

CHARLES J. BAIRD,

WHOLESALE AND RETAIL

GROCER AND WINE MERCHANT,

221 ST. JAMES STREET,

MONTREAL.

GIBB & CO.,
ESTABLISHED 1775.

Merchant Tailors,
AND

Gentlemen's Haberdashers.

148 St. James Street,   MONTREAL,

Opposite St. Lawrence Hall.

THE MEDICAL HALL,
Opposite the Post Office and corner of St. Lawrence Hall Building,

129 ST. JAMES STREET, MONTREAL,
IMPORTERS OF

Genuine Drugs, Chemicals, Perfumery,
&c., &c.

Lubin's Choice Perfumery, English Perfumery and Hair Brushes, English Toilet Soaps, Fine Turkey Sponges, Farina Cologne, Genuine, in plain and wicker bottles.

EVERY ARTICLE WARRANTED GENUINE.

Fine Old Brandy and Wines for medicinal Purposes.

Remember the address, the corner shop, below St. Lawrence Hall.

KENNETH CAMPBELL & CO.

ESTABLISHED 1818.

SAVAGE, LYMAN & CO.,
271 Notre Dame Street,
MONTREAL.

Largest Assortment of Watches in the Dominion.
Fine Jewellery in all Varieties.
Travelling Clocks, Fine Pocket Cutlery.
Travelling Bags and Cases Fitted complete.
All kinds of Fine Jewellery made to order on short notice.
Chain-making a Specialty.
Sole Agents for the celebrated Ulysse Nardin Watch.
The above Watch took the First Prize at the National Observatory for 1868 and 1869.

J. A. JOHNSTON,
MERCHANT TAILOR,
237 St. James Street,
MONTREAL.

EVERY FACILITY FOR
Executing Orders in the Latest Styles,
AND AT THE SHORTEST NOTICE.
Prices Uniform and Moderate.

W. NOTMAN,
PHOTOGRAPHER TO THE QUEEN
AND THE
EMPEROR OF FRANCE,
MONTREAL, OTTAWA, TORONTO, and HALIFAX.

NOTMAN & FRASER,
120 KING STREET EAST,
TORONTO.

PORTRAITS

Of Every Description taken in Superior Style.

WILLIAM NOTMAN

Invites Tourists to inspect the varied and extensive collection of Photographs and other Pictures which are to be seen at his Studio and the various branches as above.

Special attention is requested to his New Style of Photo-relievo Portraits, and enlarged coloured Photographs, both in Water Color and Oil.

It is not needful to remain for the completion of such orders, as they can be sent by Book post or Express to any part of the Continent or Europe.

PATRONIZED BY

H. R. H. Prince Arthur,  Prince Napoleon,

And Gentry of Montreal.

TRADE MARK.

ESTABLISHED 1847.

JOHN PALMER,
Hair Dresser, Wig Maker & Perfumer,
Importer of
HUMAN HAIR, &C.,
SWITCHES AND CHIGNONS IN EVERY VARIETY.
A LARGE ASSORTMENT OF
The Finest English and French Perfumery,
HOT AND COLD BATHS,
357 NOTRE DAME STREET,
Rear entrance St. James St., opposite St. Lawrence Hall, Montreal.
Tourists are respectfully requested to call and examine our Stock.

ESTABLISHED 1849.

BRITISH AND FOREIGN LACES AND EMBROIDERIES.

Strangers visiting Montreal are respectfully invited to visit

THE LACE HOUSE,

(280 NOTRE DAME Street, adjoining Merrill's, and opposite the Fur Establishment of John Henderson & Co.,)

Where they will find every description of **PURE LACE** from the simple to the most costly production.

WM. McDUNNOUGH,
SUCCESSOR TO JAMES PARKIN,

BRITISH AND FOREIGN LACE HOUSE,
280 NOTRE DAME STREET.

THE RECOLLET HOUSE,
CORNER OF ST. HELEN AND NOTRE DAME STREETS,
MONTREAL.

BROWN & CLAGGETT,
WHOLESALE AND RETAIL

IMPORTERS OF

Silks, Velvets, Poplins, Shawls, Mantles, and Fancy Goods.

Always on hand a Splendid Stock of

Alexandre's, Jouvin's, Josephine & Fromarit's
FRENCH KID GLOVES.

Strangers and Tourists should not fail to visit this Renowned Establishment.

The Canadian Express Company

Forwards Merchandise, Money, and Packages of every description, collects Bills with Goods, Drafts, Notes, &c., throughout the Dominion, the United States and Europe, running daily (Sundays excepted) over the entire lines of the Grand Trunk, St. Lawrence and Ottawa, Brockville and Ottawa, and Port Hope and Lindsay Railways, in charge of Special Messengers, also by the Montreal Ocean Steamship Company's Steamers to and from all parts of Europe. Expresses to and from Europe made up weekly in connection with all Railways in England, and the principal Express Company in Europe. Packages handed in at any Railway Station in England, or to the Globe Parcels Express Company at any of their offices, consigned to the care of the CANADIAN EXPRESS COMPANY, LIVERPOOL, will find quick dispatch.

LOW RATES AND LARGE CONSIGNMENTS.

PRINCIPAL OFFICES AND AGENTS:

MONTREAL,...D. T. Irish. KINGSTON,.....G. P. Oliver.
PORTLAND,...J. E. Prindle. TORONTO,...J. D. Irwin.
OTTAWA,.......C. C. Ray. DETROIT,........W. A. Gray.
QUEBEC,.......W. C. Scott. LIVERPOOL,.W. Blackwood.

Office, 22 Tower Building, Water St.

G. CHENEY, *Superintendent.*

ESTABLISHED 1834.

JOHN HENDERSON & CO.,
FURRIERS,

IMPORTERS and MANUFACTURERS of the CHOICEST

Russian and Hudson Bay Furs,

CRYSTAL BLOCK,

NO. 283 NOTRE DAME ST.
MONTREAL.

Tourists are invited to call and see our Stock on view during the Summer, embracing the

Finest Classes of Furs,

And manufactured in the very best manner.

INDIAN CURIOSITIES

AND

FANCY GOODS,

WHOLESALE AND RETAIL.

K

Grand Trunk Railway of Canada

AND

MONTREAL OCEAN  STEAMSHIP COMPANY

1870.   **WEEKLY LINE.**   **1870.**

GREAT FREIGHT ROUTE

BETWEEN

EUROPE AND NORTH AMERICA.

The MONTREAL OCEAN STEAMSHIP COMPANY'S LINE of powerful Screw Steamers will, during the SUMMER, make

SEMI-WEEKLY TRIPS BETWEEN LIVERPOOL AND MONTREAL,

And also will FORM A WEEKLY LINE BETWEEN GLASGOW and MONTREAL, there connecting with the GRAND TRUNK RAILWAY, thus forming the

MOST DIRECT ROUTE TO AND FROM ENGLAND AND THE WESTERN STATES OF THE UNION.

ONLY TWO TRANSHIPMENTS

BETWEEN LIVERPOOL AND CHICAGO, OR CINCINNATI,

GOODS SENT THROUGH IN BOND.

For Rates and other information apply to
GRAND TRUNK RAILWAY COMPANY'S OFFICE, 21 Old Broad Street, London.
MONTGOMERIE & GREENHORN, Montreal Ocean Steamship Co.'s Office, London.
ALLAN BROTHERS & Co., Weaver Buildings, Brunswick Street, Liverpool.
JAMES & ALEXANDER ALLAN, No. 70 Clyde Street, Glasgow.
S. E. MARTIN, Agent Grand Trunk Railway, Detroit, Michigan.
W. C. CAMPBELL, Acting Agent Grand Trunk Railway, Chicago, Illinois.
TAYLOR & BROTHER, Agent Grand Trunk Railway, Cincinnati, Ohio.
JOHN H. MUIR, Agent Grand Trunk Railway, Milwaukee, Wisconsin.
———, Agent Grand Trunk Railway, St. Louis, Missouri.
J. WHITMORE, Agent Grand Trunk Railway, Buffalo, New York.

H. & A. ALLAN,
  Montreal Ocean Steamship Company, Montreal, P. Q.
F. C. STRATTON, General Eastern Freight Agent,
  Grand Trunk Railway Company, Montreal, P. Q.
P. S. STEVENSON, General Western Freight Agent,
  Grand Trunk Railway Company, Toronto, P. O.

C. J. BRYDGES,
MANAGING DIRECTOR,
Grand Trunk Railway.

GODERICH AND SOUTHAMPTON LINE.

1870.  1870.

Shortest, Cheapest and Most Direct Route.

THE NEW PROPELLER

"W. SEYMOUR,"

CAPT. D. ROWAN,

Will Ply, in connection with the Grand Trunk Railway, between

Goderich and Southampton,

Leaving Goderich after the arrival of the Express Train, Touching at Kincardine, Inverhuron and Port Elgin,

EVERY DAY excepting FRIDAYS and SUNDAYS.

Forwarders for the Transaction of Freight Business at the Ports mentioned.

Tickets for Sale on the Boat for all Points in the Province and the United States.

For further information apply

WM. SEYMOUR & CO.,
GODERICH, ONT.

ADVERTISEMENTS.

1870. TO 1870.
TOURISTS AND PLEASURE SEEKERS.

IMPROVED ARRANGEMENT.

CANADIAN NAVIGATION COMPANY'S LINES
OF THROUGH STEAMERS.

Niagara Falls to Montreal, Quebec, White Mountains, Portland, Lake George, Saratoga, New York, Riviere du Loup, the River Saguenay, &c., &c., &c.

The Canadian Navigation Company's Steamers comprise the original Royal Mail and American Lines, with the addition of several new Steamers, thus forming two first-class lines of Passenger Steamers, which, for speed, safety and comfort, cannot be surpassed. They are the only lines now affording Tourists an opportunity to view the magnificent scenery of the Thousand Islands and Rapids of the St. Lawrence, also to the far famed River Saguenay.

☞ This Route possesses peculiar advantages over any other, as by it parties **have their choice of either side of Lake Ontario and River St. Lawrence, between Niagara Falls and Quebec,** over the whole or any portion of it, without being obliged to decide when purchasing their tickets; as they are also good by the Grand Trunk Railway. No extra charge for *Meals* and *State-rooms* on the Steamers between Toronto and Montreal.

The only route to the White Mountains by which parties can ascend the far-famed Mount Washington by the carriage road.

American money taken at par for tickets by this line, which can be obtained at most of the principal cities in the United States.

E. BARBER,	ALEX. MILLOY,
Agent,	*Secy. C. N. Company,*
Niagara Falls, N. Y.	Office St. James St., Montreal.

THE
OTTAWA RIVER
Navigation Company's Mail Steamers
1870.

Montreal to Ottawa City Daily
(SUNDAYS EXCEPTED.)

THE SPLENDID FAST STEAMERS

Prince of Wales,  Queen Victoria,

Capt. H. W. SHEPHERD,   Capt. A. BOWIE.

Tourists will find this a Delightful Trip.

A Train leaves Bonaventure Station every Morning (except Sunday), at Seven o'clock, to connect at Lachine with Steamer

PRINCE OF WALES,
(BREAKFAST.)

Calling at the different Landings.

From Carillon, by Railway, to Grenville, to join the

QUEEN VICTORIA,
(DINNER.)

Arrive at Ottawa City 6.00 P.M.

DOWNWARDS.

Steamer QUEEN VICTORIA leaves OTTAWA CITY at 7 A.M., passengers arriving in Montreal 5.30 P.M.

Office : 10 St. Bonaventure Street.

R. W. SHEPHERD,
President.

N.B.—Baggage Checked through.

MONTREAL,

BURNETT & DOYLE,

PROPRIETORS.

The undersigned respectfully inform their numerous friends and patrons in Canada and the United States that, by the recent enlargement and improvements effected in this establishment, they are now prepared to accommodate over 350 Guests. The Ottawa Hotel covers the entire space of ground running between St. James and Notre Dame Streets, and has two beautiful fronts; the one on the right in the above cut, represents the front on Notre Dame Street, the other on the left, the St. James Street front. The house has been thoroughly re-fitted and furnished with every regard to comfort and luxury; has hot and cold water, with baths and closets, on each floor. The aim has been to make this the most unexceptionable First-Class Hotel in Montreal. Mr. BURNETT trusts that his long experience in First-Class Hotels in New York City and the United States will give confidence to his friends and the travelling public that they will receive every comfort and attendance at the Ottawa. Notwithstanding the large outlay in furnishing, frescoeing, and other extensive improvements, the charges per day hereafter will be two dollars and a-half. Carriages with attentive drivers may be had at all times by application at the Office. Coaches will also be found at the Railway Depot and Steamboat Landings on the arrival of the several Trains and Steamers.

D. C. BURNETT, THOMAS DOYLE.
Late Proprietor of Woodruff House.
Watertown, N. Y.,
and St. James Hotel, Montreal.

ST. LAWRENCE HALL,

SITUATED ON ST. JAMES STREET, MONTREAL.

H. HOGAN, · · · · · · · · · · · · **Proprietor.**

THIS FIRST-CLASS HOTEL (the largest in Montreal) is situated on ST. JAMES STREET, in the immediate vicinity of the French Cathedral, or Church "Ville Marie," Notre Dame Street, adjoining the Post Office, Place d'Armes and Banks; is only one minute's walk from Grey or Black Nunneries, new Court House, Reading Rooms, Champ de Mars, (where the troops are reviewed), Mechanics' Institute, Bonsecours Market, and Fashionable Stores. The new Theatre Royal is directly in rear of the House, and several of the best boxes are regularly kept for Guests of this Hotel.

The **ST. LAWRENCE HALL** has long been regarded as the most popular and fashionable Hotel in Montreal, and is patronized by the Government on all public occasions, including that of the visit of His Royal Highness the Prince of Wales and suite, and that of His Excellency the Governor General and suite. During the past winter, the Hotel has been considerably enlarged, so that in future the Proprietor hopes to be able to accommodate comfortably all who may favour him with their patronage. All Rooms lighted by gas. The Consulate Office of the United States is in the Hotel, as well as Telegraph Office to all parts. The Proprietor begs to announce that having recently purchased the **ST. LAWRENCE HALL** Property, it is his intention next fall to pull down and rebuild it with all the modern improvements, including an Elevator; thus making this Hotel second to none in the United States.

Montreal, May, 1870.

St. James Hotel,

MONTREAL.

The undersigned beg to notify the Public that they have Purchased the above well known FIRST-CLASS HOTEL, and which is now carried on as a BRANCH ESTABLISHMENT of the ST. LAWRENCE HALL, under the management of Mr. SAMUEL MONTGOMERY, (Nephew of Mr. HOGAN,) and Mr. FREDERICK GERIKEN, both well-known to the Travelling Community, both in the United States and Canada, as being connected with the ST. LAWRENCE HALL.

The ST. JAMES is very favorably situated, facing Victoria Square, in the very centre of the City, and contiguous to the Post Office and the Banks. Its convenience for Business Men is everything that can be desired, as it is in the immediate vicinity of the leading Wholesale Houses. THE Rooms being well appointed and ventilated, are cheerful for families; while the ménage will always be unexceptionable, and no pains spared in ministering to the comfort of Guests. The Proprietors, having leased the adjoining premises, are prepared to offer every inducement to the Spring and Fall trade; and as their tariff is unexceptionably reasonable, they hope to obtain a large share of public patronage.

H. HOGAN & CO.

ALBION HOTEL.

McGILL AND ST. PAUL STREETS.
MONTREAL, CANADA.

For twenty years past this Hotel has been the favorite resort of the general travelling public in the United States as well as Canada when visiting Montreal on business or pleasure. Alterations, additions and improvements have been at different times inaugurated to keep pace with the requirements of such an extended patronage. The house has been newly furnished throughout, and, in the working out of the many alterations that have lately taken place, due attention has been given to everything which would conduce to the comfort of guests.

The ALBION HOTEL of Montreal is now one of the largest Hotels in the Dominion, having ample accommodation for 500 guests.

Great as the changes are, that have lately been made, no additional charge will be made. The charge will be $1.50 per day as heretofore. The travelling community will consult their own interests by remembering the ALBION HOTEL when visiting Montreal.

LIFE INSURANCE

AND

Accident Insurance

BY THE

Travelers' Insurance Co.

OF HARTFORD, CONN.

Cash Assets, $1,250,000.

Life and Endowment Policies in this Company combine ample security and cheapness of cost, under a definite contract. Its low cash rates are equivalent to a dividend in advance.

The only Accident Insurance Company issuing yearly policies. Has paid to its policy-holders over **$1,000,000** for Death or Injury by Accident.

JAS. G. BATTERSON,	RODNEY DENNIS,
President.	*Secretary.*
GEO. B. LESTER,	CHAS. E. WILSON,
Actuary.	*Assistant Secretary.*

AGENCIES in all the principal Towns and Cities in Canada.

MONTREAL OFFICE, 241 ST. JAMES STREET.

T. E. FOSTER,
General Agent.

Citizens' Insurance Company
(OF CANADA.)

LIFE DEPARTMENT,

This Company, formed by the Association of nearly 100 of the wealthiest and most influential Citizens of Montreal, is especially empowered by Act of Parliament, and is also **Authorized by the Government**, under the provisions of the Insurance Bill.

Policies are issued on ALL THE MODERN PLANS, including

Limited Payments, Endowments Part Cash and Part Credit Premiums without notes, Income Producing System, and several new and valuable plans.

A comparison of the very Low Rates, and of the liberal and unrestrictive nature of this Company's Policies with those of any other Company, is especially invited.

All Life Policies are absolutely Non-Forfeitable.

Persons intending to assure their lives are particularly requested to first examine the prospectus of this Company, which together with all information concerning the working of the various plans may be obtained at the

Head Office, No. 175 St. James St., Montreal.

EDWARD RAWLINGS,
Manager.

Royal Insurance Company,
FIRE AND LIFE.

Capital, - - - - - - - - - £2,000,000 Stg.
Annual Income over, - - - - - 800,000 "
Accumulated Funds invested exceed, 1,600,000 "

The ROYAL has never amalgamated with any other Company. Has deposited, in compliance with the recent Act of the Legislature of the Dominion of Canada, the sum of $150,000 for the security of the Canadian Insurers.

FIRE BRANCH.
Very Moderate Rates of Premium.
Prompt and Liberal Settlement of Losses.
Loss and Damage by Explosion of Gas made good.
No Charge for Policies or Transfers.

LIFE BRANCH.
Perfect Security to Assurers.
Moderate Rates of Premium.
Large Participation of Profits—the Bonuses being amongst the Largest hitherto declared by any Office, and Divided every Five Years.
Exemption of Assured from Liability of Partnership.
Claims settled promptly on Proof of Death.
Liberal Allowance for Surrendered Policies.
Forfeiture of Policy cannot take place from Unintentional Mis-statement.
No Charge for Policies or Assignments.
Medical Fees paid by the Company.

Tables and Forms of Application, with all other Information, can be obtained by application to

H. L. ROUTH,
Agent, MONTREAL.

W. E. SCOTT, *Medical Examiner*, } MONTREAL.
ALFRED PERRY, *Fire Inspector*, }

Particular attention is requested to this Company's New Life Assurance Scheme.

PERRY, NIMMO & CO.,
MANUFACTURERS OF
Saratoga, Imperial and Eugenie Trunks, Solid Leather Trunks, Portmanteaux and Valises, Bags, Satchels, &c., Wholesale and Retail.
371 NOTRE DAME STREET, MONTREAL.
P. S.—Repairs will receive prompt attention.

Established 1830. | **DAVID LEVY,** | Established 1830.

SUCCESSOR TO THE LATE SIMON LEVY,

Importer of

JEWELLERY, PLATE, PLATED WARE,
CHINA, GLASS AND FANCY GOODS,
1 JOHN STREET, QUEBEC.

D. L. has constantly on hand and receives direct from Europe all the latest novelties in

FINE GOLD JEWELLERY,
 HANDSOME ORNAMENTS AND VASES,
  RICH ENGRAVED CUT GLASS,
   E. P. TEA AND COFFEE SETS, URNS, KETTLES,
    CRUET STANDS, CAKE BASKETS,
     BISCUIT BOXES, PICKLE STANDS,
      EPERGNES, SIDE PIECES, &c., &c.,

In all comprising one of the largest and best selected Stocks to be seen in any one house in the Dominion of Canada.

O'DOHERTY & CO.,
18 FABRIQUE STREET, QUEBEC,
GENERAL IMPORTERS OF

FANCY and STAPLE DRY GOODS,
OLD ESTABLISHED HOUSE FOR

Best Lyons Black Silks, Fancy Silks, Moire Antiques, Irish Poplins, Rich Genoa Velvets, Real Thread Laces, French Cambric and Lace Bordered Handkerchiefs, Lace Collars and Cuffs, &c., &c.,

And Domestic Goods of every description direct from the Manufacturers.

ONLY ONE PRICE.

O'DOHERTY & CO.,
18 FABRIQUE STREET,
Quebec.

LEGER & RINFRET,
IMPORTERS OF

English and French Dry Goods,
21 FABRIQUE STREET,
UPPER TOWN, QUEBEC.

N. B.—Latest novelties received per every Mail Steamer:

BLACK and COLOURED FRENCH SILKS, LACES, COLLARS and CUFFS.

PARASOLS EN TOUT CAS, AND UMBRELLAS, SILK, LISLE THREAD, BALLERIGAN HOSIERY IN GREAT VARIETY.

ALEXANDER'S and MORIGANT'S KID GLOVES.

GENTLEMEN'S DEPARTMENT.

White and Coloured Shirts, Hosiery and Gloves, Collars, Ties, Underclothing, Tweeds and Cloth, and Gentlemen's suits made to order.

SEA BATHING.

ST. LAWRENCE HALL,
CACOUNA.

THIS ESTABLISHMENT has been considerably ENLARGED during the past winter, and is now capable of affording accommodation for SIX HUNDRED GUESTS. Additional land has been purchased and laid out in Pleasure Grounds; it is beautifully situated on the Banks of the St. Lawrence, commanding a fine view of the River; and the Steamers and Vessels pass up and down in close proximity to the place. The BATHING accommodation has also been much improved. Billiard Tables, Bowling Alleys, &c., &c., &c., on the premises. Instrumental Band always in attendance. There is a Telegraph Office in the Hotel, an advantage not possessed by any place on the North Shore; and, with the advantage of Railroad and Steamboat conveyance daily, it stands unrivalled by any other place of the description in Canada. It is superfluous to say more in its favor than the fact that a number of the most prominent citizens of the Provinces have built beautiful residences, and occupy them during the Summer months: probably not less than THREE THOUSAND people are located here in various cottages. There are three different places of public worship in the village. Stabling has been erected on the premises, enabling parties to keep their own Horses and Carriages at reasonable rates. The Proprietor has also arranged with Mr. VILLIERS, of Quebec, to take down a Stable of Horses, and give riding lessons daily; he has a number of Side Saddles for the use of Ladies. In fact, no pains have been spared to render this place a favorite resort during the winter months. Liberal arrangements will be made with parties remaining the whole or part of the Season. Transient visitors charged at the rate of $2.50 per day.

Messrs. SHIPMAN, JUNR., & KENLEY,

May, 1870.   MANAGERS.

SUMMER ARRANGEMENT.

1870.  1870.

OPENING OF THE

Great Favorite Route

VIA

MONTREAL AND PLATTSBURGH,

•Rutland and Burlington, Rensselaer and Saratoga Railroads,

AND

LAKE CHAMPLAIN STEAMERS,

52 Miles shorter to NEW YORK, 18 Miles shorter to BOSTON,
THAN BY ANY OTHER ROUTE.

TWO EXPRESS TRAINS DAILY FROM MONTREAL.

On and after MONDAY, 2nd May, Trains will run as follows, from Grand Trunk Depot, Bonaventure Station:

MORNING EXPRESS, 6 A. M.

For Plattsburgh, Burlington, Rutland, Whitehall, Saratoga, Troy, Schenectady, Albany, Bellowes Falls, Northampton, Springfield, Hartford, New Haven, New London, Norwich, Keene, Fitchburg, Lowell, Worcester, Boston and New York, arriving in BOSTON at 6.30 P.M., NEW YORK 9.50 P. M.

EVENING EXPRESS, 4 P. M.

For Plattsburgh, Burlington, Rutland, Whitehall, Saratoga, Troy, Schenectady, Albany, Bellowes Falls, Northampton, Springfield, Hartford, New Haven, New London, Norwich, Keene, Fitchburg, Lowell, Worcester, Boston and New York, arriving in BOSTON at 8.30 A. M., NEW YORK at 11 A.M.

Passengers by this Route leaving MONTREAL at 6.00 A.M, will reach PLATTSBURG at 8.30 A.M. there connecting with the elegant Steamers of the CHAMPLAIN TRANSPORTATION COMPANY, on board which they Breakfast, and enjoy two hours rail over the most interesting portion of Lake Champlain, connecting at BURLINGTON with RUTLAND and BURLINGTON RAILROAD, at RUTLAND with RENSSELAER and SARATOGA RAILROAD, at TROY with HUDSON RIVER RAILROAD and TROY STEAMBOAT CO., also at Albany with PEOPLES' LINE of Steamers. The only DAY TRAIN between MONTREAL and NEW YORK is over this line, arriving in NEW YORK at 9.50 P.M. No change of Cars between Montreal and Plattsburgh. Maps and Time Bills of the Route furnished at the Office.

Elegant Smoking Cars on all Day Trains. Splendid Sleeping Cars on all Night Trains. Baggage checked through and examined by U. S. Custom Officer before leaving Montreal. For Tickets and further information apply at the General Union Ticket Office, No. 143 St. James Street, adjoining St. Lawrence Hall.

R. CARDINAL, Agent.

FOUQUET'S HOTEL,
Plattsburgh, N. Y.

This Hotel is situated at Plattsburgh, upon the Western Shore of LAKE CHAMPLAIN, on the banks of Cumberland Bay, which was the scene of the naval battle of 1814. Fine views can be had from its piazzas in all directions, which include the Lake, the Islands, the Green Mountains on the East, the Adirondacks on the South, presenting every variety of scenery, the wild, the picturesque, the grand. This Hotel is retired, it has beautiful garden and flower grounds, purest of spring water, spacious and well ventilated rooms, which together with the pleasant drives in the vicinity, offer attractions to the seeker after health and pleasure that cannot be surpassed.

To See Lake Champlain and Lake George by Daylight,

Leave Montreal by the afternoon Train and arrive at FOUQUET'S HOTEL to supper; take day boat the following day for Whitehall, or Lake George, arrive at Saratoga via Whithall, to supper.

For Lake George,

Leave the Steamer at Ticonderoga, thence by Stage four miles around the rapids to Lake George, thence by Steamer MINNE.HA-HA to Caldwell at the upper end of the Lake, at which place are the ruins of Fort William Henry, of Revolutionary fame.

By this arrangement the Tourist has the advantage of passing by daylight through the entire length of two of the most noted sheets of water in America, seeing all their varied beauty and portions connected with them, both historical and romantic.

New Route to the Adirondacks.

THE WHITEHALL AND PLATTSBURGH RAILROAD is now completed and being operated from Plattsburgh to Ausable River Station, a distance of twenty miles, connecting with a four horse line of Stages, running daily to the principal summer resorts of the GREAT WILDERNESS. Tickets for this route can be procured at the principal Ticket-Offices, on the Lake Champlain Steamers and at this Hotel.

L

TO THE TRAVELLER

"EN ROUTE"

From Niagara, Ogdensburgh, Montreal, Quebec,

TO

BURLINGTON, MT. MANSFIELD, TICONDEROGA, LAKE GEORGE, SARATOGA, TROY, ALBANY, NEW YORK, SPRINGFIELD AND BOSTON.

The Established route via PLATTSBURGH and LAKE CHAMPLAIN offers the Tourists and Business men attractions possessed by no other Line, combining as it does LESS CHANGES than any other, and scenery more picturesque, historical and romantic, than can be found in any other part of the American continent in the same distance.

TWO TRAINS DAILY leave MONTREAL and OGDENSBURGH, connecting at PLATTSBURGH with the elegant and commodious steamers of the

CHAMPLAIN TRANSPORTATION CO.,

ADIRONDACK.....................Capt. Wm. H. Flagg,
CANADA............................ " Anderson,
UNITED STATES................. " J. C. Babbitt,

forming TWO DAILY LINES, each way through the Lake, connecting at BURLINGTON with trains of Rutland Railroad, for all Eastern points, at TICONDEROGA with Steamer "Minne-ha-ha," through LAKE GEORGE, and at WHITEHALL with trains of Rensselaer and Saratoga Railroad for SARATOGA, TROY, ALBANY, NEW YORK, and all Southern and Western points.

From Plattsburgh, the point of embarkation, to Whitehall, a distance of one hundred miles, the traveller witnesses on either side a continuous chain of beautiful mountain scenery. This, with the historical interest connected with this delightful sheet of water, makes this route both interesting and attractive.

The Steamers of the Line are, as they always have been, models of neatness and comfort, and every attention is paid by their officers to the patrons of the Line.

The ONLY route to Lake George, and only direct route to Saratoga.

THROUGH TICKETS,

And information, can be obtained at the Ticket Offices, at Niagara Falls, at the Company's Office, 143 St. James Street, Montreal, (adjoining St. Lawrence Hall,) at the Offices of Grand Trunk Railway, on board of Steamers, and at the General Office of the Company, Burlington, Vt.

May, 1870

The Welden House.

ST. ALBANS, VT.

This favorite house has lately undergone very thorough repairs and alterations, and a large addition made to its heretofore generous capacity; including a Ladies' ordinary, Ladies' Billiard Room and spacious Croquet Grounds; the comfort of its guests having been studied, by making large and airy rooms, with all the modern improvements of a first-class hotel.

This house contains over two hundred rooms, and is situated on the Vermont Central and Vermont and Canada Railroads, the great thoroughfare from New York and Boston to Montreal and the West. Its location for a summer resort is all that could be desired, affording all the benefits of the mountain air, combined with the cool and refreshing winds from Lake Champlain.

The "Panoramic Views" from St. Albans are unequalled either on this continent or the old, as is often stated by Tourists.

In addition to the above attractions are the wonderful mineral waters of Franklin County, the fame of which is making it the Germany of the New World. The Health-giving waters of the "Welden Spring" are furnished free to the Guests. Terms $3.50 per day. A liberal discount will be made to Summer Boarders.

WALTER McDONALD, Proprietor

Vermont Central Railway,

SHORTEST AND MOST DIRECT ROUTE FOR

New York, Boston, White and Green Mountains, Lakes Champlain and George.

THE ONLY LINE RUNNING

Magnificent Drawing Room Cars, and Silver Palace Sleeping Cars.

Baggage examined at Montreal by Customs' Officer and checked through.

TICKETS, STATEROOMS and SEATS in DRAWING ROOM CARS, and BERTHS in SLEEPING CARS, with full and reliable information, can be obtained at the COMPANY'S OFFICE, No. 136 ST. JAMES STREET, opposite St. Lawrence Hall, Montreal.

L. MILLIS, General Agent.　　　　**F. PICARD,**
No. 5 State Street, Boston.　　　　Ticket Agent.

PRINCE OF WALES SALOON,

Opposite Grand Trunk Railway Station,

BELLEVILLE, ONTARIO,

WM. DOCTER, Proprietor.

Choicest WINES, LIQUORS and ALES always on hand.

UNITED STATES HOTEL,

PORTLAND, MAINE.

This Hotel has long been known to the travelling public as one of the most popular public houses in New England. It is situated in the square in the heart of the beautiful City of Portland. In point of location it is confessedly superior to any Hotel in the City. Its appointments are all first-class, and its table and attendance will always be found all that the public can desire, while its terms are reasonable. In a word it is a first-class Hotel upon second rate terms. The House has been placed in complete order for the season of 1870, and the Proprietors invite the public patronage, confident of being able to please in the future as in the past.

GIBSON, BURRILL & CO.

PORTLAND, BANGOR

AND

MACHIAS STEAMBOAT COMPANY.

 1870.

SUMMER ARRANGEMENT

The Steamer **CITY OF RICHMOND**, WILLIAM E. DENNISON, Master, will Leave Railroad Wharf, foot State Street, Portland, every MONDAY, WEDNESDAY and FRIDAY Evenings at 10 o'clock, or on arrival of Express Train from Boston

FOR BANGOR,

Touching at Rockland, Camden, Belfast, Searsport, Sandy Point, Bucksport, Witerport, and Hampden.

Returning, will leave BANGOR every MONDAY, WEDNESDAY and FRIDAY Mornings, at 6 o'clock, touching at the above-named landings, arriving in Portland same afternoon about half-past four o'clock.

The Favorite Steamer **"LEWISTON,"** Capt. CHARLES DEERING, Master, will leave Railroad Wharf, foot of State Street, Portland, every TUESDAY and FRIDAY Evenings, at 10 o'clock, or on arrival of Express Train from Boston

FOR MACHIAS PORT,

Touching at Rockland, Castine, Deer Isle, Sedgwick, Mount Desert, Millbridge, and Jonesport.

N. B. The *Lewiston* will land at Bar Harbor, Mount Desert, each trip from July 3rd to September 16th, in addition to her usual landings at South West Harbor.

This Steamer usually connects with Sandford's Boston and Bangor Steamers at Rockland.

Returning, will leave Machias Port every MONDAY and THURSDAY morning, at 5 o'clock, touching at the above-named landings, arriving in Portland same night.

ROSS & STURDIVANT,
GENERAL AGENTS,
Portland, May, 1870.   179 Commercial Street.

MOUNT DESERT.

One hundred and ten miles east from Portland, Maine, lies the picturesque island of MOUNT DESERT. It is eighteen miles long and about twelve in breadth, and joined to the main land by Trenton bridge. Champlain named the place "Monts Deserts" on account of its rude solitudes, and its early history is full of romantic interest.

Old chronicles tell us many a tale of ancient fisherman, priest and savage. Under the shadow of Newport Mt., the French Jesuits raised their cross, centuries ago in gratitude to God for their escape from shipwreck, and the shores of the sound have, doubtless, echoed back

"The chant of many a holy hymn
And solemn bells of vesper ringing."

Indian relics, places where gold is said to have been buried, ruins of the cellars on ancient dwellings and other objects of interest diversify the tourist's ramble among the mountain lakes, the seaside hamlets, the beetling crags or over the pleasant meadows. Since the days of the Gregories—who held property here under an old grant from LOUIS XIV, and whose graves are seen just outside the little cemetery north of Bar Harbor— the history of Mt. Desert has presented less of historic romance.

Latterly, however, the place has enjoyed a growing celebrity as a healthful summer resort. Its scenery is unequalled in variety, presenting in the same neighborhood, as one has suggested, "the Isle of Shoals and Wachusett, Nahant and Monadnock, Newport and the Catskills." The hurried traveller carries away only the grander, awe inspiring features of the island, but a more intimate acquaintance, reveals its tenderer elements of beauty ;

"Winding shores
Of narrow capes and isles which lie
Slumbering to Ocean's Lullaby."

No visitor can ever forget "the quiet charm of the coves at the head of the sound, the mill in the meadow under Dry Mt. and the merry brook below it; the pebbly beach north of Bar Island, the long bright way beyond, and the soft ripple of the waves dying in harmony with the murmur of the pines ; calm sunrises over quiet seas, broad moon-light on shining forests, glowing sunsets across purpling distance, and tender after-glow on shadowy hills complete the radiant changes of the days.

One would feign linger till the autumnal breezes fill the air, and the October splendor lights up the valleys. July will perhaps furnish all the requisites of good weather before the dog-days begin."

Approaching from Portland, the first landing point on Mt. Desert is South-west harbor on the lower side of the Sound. Here is the Island House, kept by H. H. Clark, who furnishes carriages, boats, guides and every facility and comfort to his guests. The Freeman House and Ocean House are in the same neighborhood.

Bowling alleys and bathing houses are also open. Delightful drives and rambles may be had, especially northward round the head of Somes Sound which nearly bisects the island. Leaving Somesville, the tourist will, by an hour's drive, reach the westerly slope of Green Mt. about 1800 feet high. A road leads to the summit. Of the exquisite beauty of the scene thus presented, Whittier has given a picture in the legend of his "Mogg Megone." At Bar Harbor, 15 miles from S. W. Harbor, there is the Agmont House, also the Harbor House, the Rodick House, and THE WAYSIDE INN, just erected by Capt. R E. Higgens, who nobly saved, at the risk of his own life, the only surviver of that party of nine who were sunk in Frenchman's Bay two years since.

The scenery about Bar Harbor is enchanting. Of the mountain and stream, island, cave and lake, with the river, bay and headland which answer to names, suggestive of tender memories, and "Whose melody yet lingers like the last vibration of the red man's requiem,"—a volume might be written.

Four miles from Bar Harbor, southerly, at Schooner Head, are Spouting Horn and the Devil's Oven, the one a cleft in the crag, through which the sea roars and spouts with terrific force, and the other a huge cavern, beautifully pictured by Miss Barnes, in her late monograph of Mt. Desert. On the broad, dank floor, enamelled with pink and pale green, are crowded strange creations of wondrous sea life, from the tiny white daisy bud, and sweet anemones, to the great, tawny creature, whose broad side, striped with amber and crimson, covers the hand.

"The sunlight reflected from the blue waves shone on the dark vault above us, as through broad chancel window down cathedral nave ; and sitting there one morning ,with wind and wave and echo for organ roll, we sang Old Hundred."

The memory of a month at MT. DESERT at the noontide of the year, is itself a summer idyl, and will combine the elements of choicest interest and most enduring pleasure

BOOKS FOR TOURISTS.

WHITE HILLS;
Their Legends, Landscape and Poetry,
BY THOMAS STARR KING.

A new and elegant edition of this superb book with over sixty illustrations on wood. Cloth ; gilt top, $3.00.
The same (with additional Photographic Illustrations from nature,)

    Turkey morocco,............$9.00
    Half-calf................. 6.00

HISTORY OF THE WHITE MOUNTAINS,

A new edition of this brought complete down to the present time, containing accounts of the early settlements of the Mountains, Indian Legends and Traditions, together with a full and accurate description of the fatal Willey Slide. These books may be obtained from the news dealers on the Roads and Steamers and the Summer hotels, or from HURD & HOUGHTON, Publishers, New York.

WHITE MOUNTAINS.
PROFILE HOUSE,
FRANCONIA NOTCH, N. H.

The PROFILE is among the largest of all the Mountain Hotels ; is unsurpassed in all its appointments and arrangements. For GRANDEUR and BEAUTY of scenery the location can not be equalled at any point in the WHITE MOUNTAINS, being in the immediate vicinity of "THE OLD MAN OF THE MOUNTAIN," "PROFILE LAKE," "ECHO LAKE," "MOUNT LAFAYETTE,"-"THE FLUME," "THE POOL," and the "BASIN." Daily Mails between New York and Boston Telegraph Office in hotel. Easy of access from all points, being only a short distance from Littleton, where passengers over B. C. and M. R. R. and Conn. and Pass River R. R. leave the Cars, reaching Profile at 2¼ and 7½ P. M. Daily Stages to all principal points in the Mountains.

Post Office Address:

TAFT & GREENLEAF,
PROFILE HOUSE, N. H.

ESTABLISHED 1835.

RENFREW & MARCOU,

(Late HENDERSON & RENFREW,)

20 BUADE STREET,

QUEBEC,

(Facing the French Cathedral.)

Tourists are invited to visit our

FUR SHOW ROOMS,

Open during the Summer, which contain one of the largest Stocks in Canada of

Hudson Bay and Russia Sables,

REAL SEALSKIN JACKETS,

Gentlemen's Furs,

SLEIGH ROBES, FUR COATS,

INDIAN CURIOSITIES,

Moose Heads, &c.

ALSO,

Best London made Umbrellas.

THE LEADING HOUSE IN CANADA,
ESTABLISHED 1838.
J. G. JOSEPH & CO., London and Paris House, Toronto.

MASONIC EMPORIUM,—JEWELS, CLOTHING, REGALIA and FURNITURE of all DESCRIPTIONS. J. G. JOSEPH & CO., King Street, Toronto.

J. G. JOSEPH & CO., Importers of FINE GOLD JEWELLERY, WATCHES, DIAMONDS, SILVER WARE and FANCY GOODS, Toronto.

ST. LOUIS HOTEL,
ST. LOUIS STREET,
AND
RUSSELL HOTEL,
PALACE STREET, QUEBEC.

THE
ST. LOUIS HOTEL,
WHICH IS UNRIVALLED FOR SIZE,
Style and Locality in Quebec,
IS OPEN ONLY DURING THE SEASON OF PLEASURE TRAVEL.

It is eligibly situated, near to, and surrounded by, the most delightful and fashionable promenades, the Governor's Garden, the Citadel, the Esplanade, the Place d'Armes, and Durham Terrace, which furnish the splendid views and magnificent scenery for which Quebec is so justly celebrated and which is unsurpassed in any part of the world.

The Proprietor, in returning thanks for the very liberal patronage he has hitherto enjoyed, inform the public, that these Hotels have been thoroughly renovated and embellished, and can now accommodate about 500 visitors; and assure them that nothing will be wanting, on his part, that will conduce to the comfort and enjoyment of his Guests.

WILLIS RUSSELL, *Proprietor.*

The correct time by which the Trains are run is supplied by J. G. JOSEPH & CO., Toronto.

www.ingramcontent.com/pod-product-compliance
Lightning Source LLC
Chambersburg PA
CBHW020253170426
43202CB00008B/346